Becoming

Right for the Heart...
Good for the Whole

Path of Potential • P.O. Box 4058, Grand Junction, CO 81502 USA

TABLE OF CONTENTS

Path of Potential • P.O. Box 4058, Grand Junction, CO 81502 USA

Becoming

Right for the Heart...
Good for the Whole

Path of Potential

Path of Potential • P.O. Box 4058, Grand Junction, CO 81502 USA

Becoming Fully and Truly Human

Manifesting and realizing
the potential enfolded within,
we become fully and truly human.

Our paths are many... and unique. They are the trace of the process by which we discover and manifest our purpose, our work, and our role: the way of our calling. Yet, there is a commonness - a oneness - that is shared by each and all:
- We all emanate from the same Source: our common Father.
- We are all people of earth: our common mother.
- We share a longing to return and a yearning to become.
- We share a common humanity and membership in the whole of life.
- We are one living family...
...and yet we have not realized our potential: the fullness and truth of our humanness... we have not yet become fully and truly human.

Open Our Hearts

For almost a decade, the people of Kennett Square, Pennsylvania have been working every day to make Kennett a better place in which to grow up and grow old. It is their hope that through the spirit and energy entering their hearts and efforts, Kennett Square might become a living seed for a world at peace. They are, each day, moving closer to realization. Their work is a grassroots process: each and all join in from the heart; they seek no outside funding; they strive to add no burden; they operate as an open free process; they focus on the potential of the people, the community, and the land.

The story of Kennett Square is here told from the heart of one woman – Joan Holliday – who generously shares her ongoing journey. This is not to say the journey has come anywhere near its end; but let us say we are pausing for a moment to take in and reflect on the awe and wonder of the vistas from the path.

Before immersing ourselves in Joan's spirited community experiences, we take time to reflect on some essential truths. It is true that one might pick up a helpful technique or promising tool from the Kennett work... but by so doing, we miss the whole point and process of their work and the philosophy behind it. Realizing our work and role in the community of life on this earth enables us to take in the fullness and wholeness of the Kennett experience, while preparing the ground for finding our own unique path and that of our community... as well as the crucial "anchor points" we must access when we are tempted to stray from our path.

Coming to grips with our membership and place in the community of life prepares us for the from-the-heart voice of Joan Holliday as she shares the every day experiences of a community of people moving toward realizing peace and wholeness. Although Joan's experiences may be unique to her and to her community, they are not unfamiliar... for we all know that when we open our hearts and are filled with aspiration, what manifests is often well beyond what we could ever imagine.

Following the stories of Kennett Square, we find food for thought as we consider and embark on building our own practical living philosophy. The importance of each of us consciously and deliberately developing and building our own living philosophy cannot be stressed enough. In the absence of an intentional philosophy of life, we are like tumbleweeds in the wind or ducks jumping on bugs – we have no direction of our own, no path we are following, no means of keeping to higher ground, no life aim; we have no purpose. A practical living philosophy is the intentional perspective we hold on the meaning of life and living... a perspective that harmonizes with the essence of the living land, and enables the unfolding of hidden and open-ended potential.

Finally, we conclude this reader with embracing the truth of our oneness. These contemplations are shared for the purpose of aiding us as we discover and choose our own unique path of potential: the work of our hearts... our way of becoming. They are written, not to provide procedural or technical information about becoming healthy working communities, but to provide food for contemplation through which we can live and work in our communities in ways that are healthy, spirited and unifying. By so doing, our hearts begin to experience what it means to become fully and truly human.

Path of Potential • P.O. Box 4058, Grand Junction, CO 81502 USA

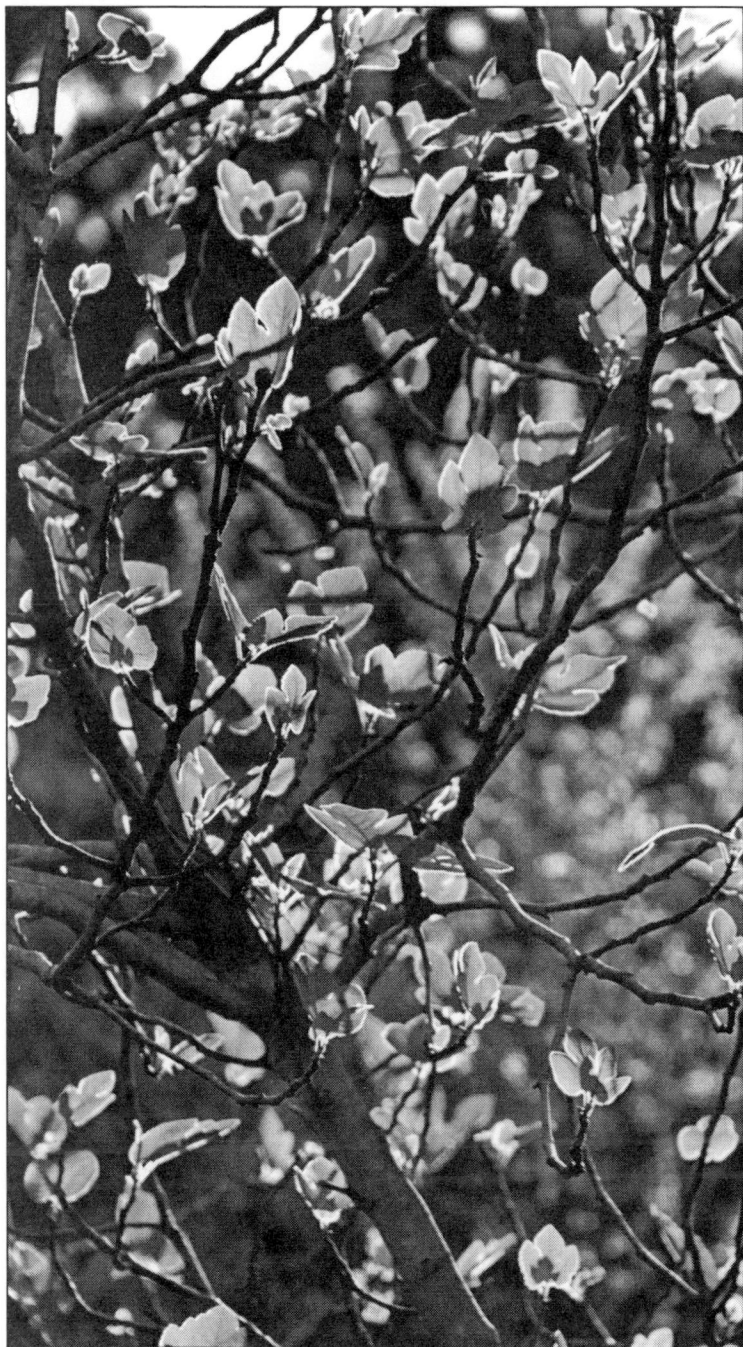

Discover Our Yearning to Become

Among a seemingly growing number of folks, there is an experiencing of an inner stirring - an awakening, a seeking, a questioning about life... our life. Is it really only about stuff and style? Is there not something deeper – more meaningful? Are we not living in increasingly coarse energies – in growing divisiveness? Should not the negativity – even among those who seem to share our views and opinions – be a source of concern? Is the path we are on truly leading to peace, harmony and rightful living?

The heart, our hearts, are being awakened and made aware. Regardless of factual argument, logical reasoning, or justified reasons, there lies within an intuitive discord – a heartfelt disturbance that reason cannot quell. This discord of the heart, when not discarded and given proper and serious attention, leads to reflection – to seeking – to a genuine desire for uncovering a new way... a seeking that, itself, leads to further reflection and, like all reflection, continues to move innerly. As our reflecting moves within, we begin to see and discover an urge – a deep yearning to become. Our yearning to become seems to be similar to and as strong as our longing to return... the longing we have to return to our Source, the Source of creation... that longing to return home to a place of peace, love and contentment, a place free of earthly struggle and foibles.

This urge, this yearning to become, is what is behind the stirring and awakening many are experiencing. This urge is a true yearning to have purpose and meaning in our lives, to have a real sense of virtue and value - a sense of being significant and of living in a way that provides a substantive answer to these com-

Path of Potential • P.O. Box 4058, Grand Junction, CO 81502 USA

monly expressed questions posed at the end of one's life: Did my life have meaning? Did I serve a purpose? Did I make a difference?

As we move even more innerly, we notice our reflecting takes on an outward orientation. We begin looking outwardly – opening our hearts to the wonder and awe of the creation before us... allowing it to freely enter and work its way into our inner self - to the very core of our being. We not only see the beauty, but begin to experience much more. What now begins to open up for us is a true experiencing of creation's ever present systemic relatedness - the intimate connection of all of life's members... the roles that are being filled, and the uncovering of the truth that we are called to be active members in the community of life. Slowly, but with deepening conviction, we can see and experience the intention and wondrous design of the whole of creation... an intent and design emanating from a common Source.

The inward and outward reflecting not only bring us real and spirit-awakening images and emotions, but bring to consciousness the realization of there being a void – a source of growthful tension within that works to cause us to seek ways of living that are more meaningful, purposeful, and intentional... ways that acknowledge our living nature and lead us to more harmonious ways of living, not only with our fellow human beings, but with our fellow creatures of life, and with life itself.

All of these reflections – the truths that we can see and make real in our hearts – come to life and inspirit us as we come to grips with perhaps the most significant truth of our becoming: We are not the source. We, like all of life, are intended and designed to be instruments of the ongoing Source of ongoing creation.

Path of Potential • P.O. Box 4058, Grand Junction, CO 81502 USA

Harmonize with Life on Earth

Becoming is a way neither led nor induced by existing structures or powers, but one that is truly grassroots... a way neither predetermined nor prescribed by experts, but one that is unfolding... a way that is lit up through spirit entering open hearts such that roles can be seen and taken on – roles that are right for the heart and good for the whole. Yes, becoming fully and truly human is an unprescribed way, but one that – if we wish to discover and follow it – demands a particular orientation.

Becoming requires an embracement of the truth of our design: We are intentionally created as members in the community of life, designed and intended to "tune into" and live harmoniously with the virtue of the land upon which we live and work. By tuning into the virtue of the land, we are more able to transcend divisive differences, celebrate uniquenesses, and, through community, experience and generate wholeness – the aim and expression of the truth of our oneness.

Path of Potential • P.O. Box 4058, Grand Junction, CO 81502 USA

Realizing Our Work
and Role
on this Earth

*If our wish and our aim is to live harmoniously
with earth while pursuing a path of realizing
potential as we follow the work of our hearts, we
will find much value and food for reflection in
these essential truths.*

*Earth
belongs to the
Creator;*

*we -
humankind -
are people of
earth.*

14

Earth is our mother;
yet she, like we, like all of life
and its members, emanate from
a common Source...
the ongoing
Source of creation.

Earth was created to
have a place
for life to enter
into the working
of the universe.

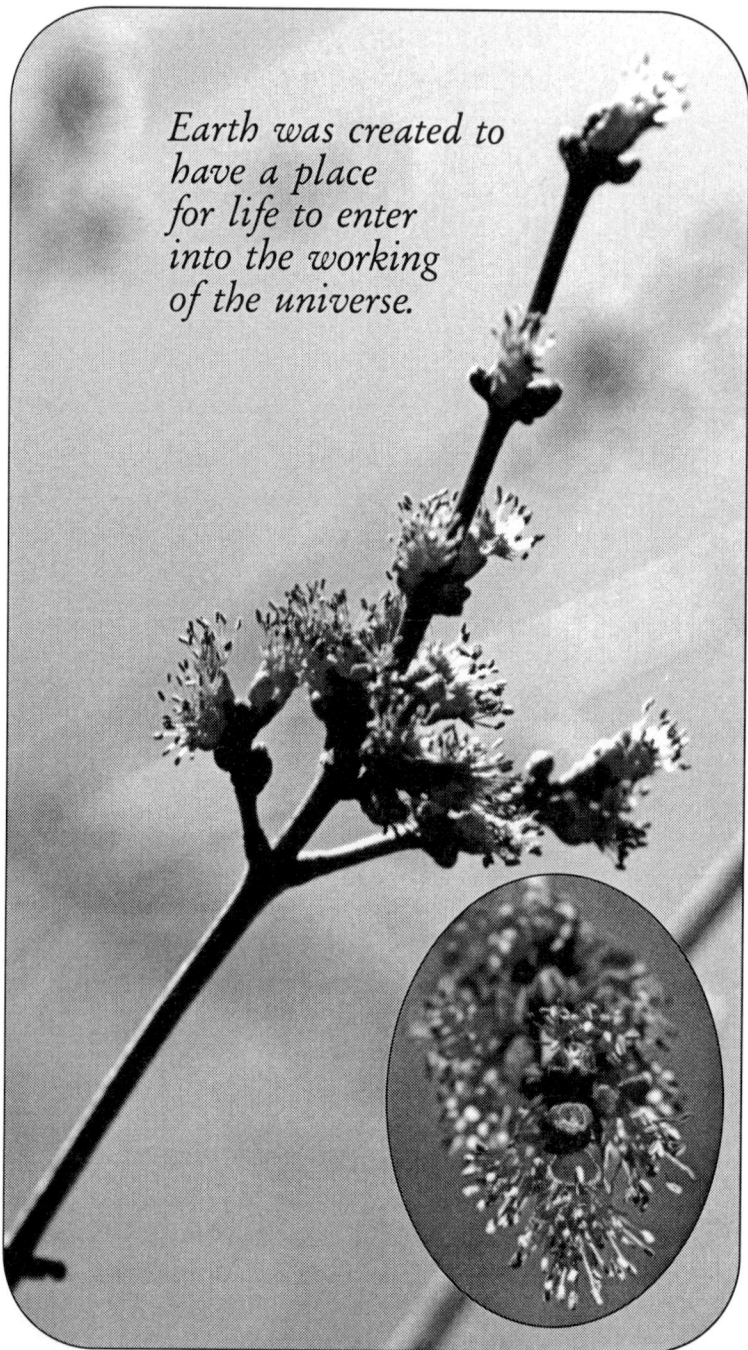

Path of Potential • P.O. Box 4058, Grand Junction, CO 81502 USA

Earth was
not intended
to be a place
for a meager
expression
of life,
but rather a
place where
life is to
flourish,
develop
and
evolve...

...a
vibrant
and vital
place...
a home
teeming
with life.

Earth is a sacred space
where life works
to establish
and sustain
its presence and
its willful receptivity
to the life force.

Path of Potential • P.O. Box 4058, Grand Junction, CO 81502 USA

*The life force is a particular
manifestation of the love
of the Creator.*

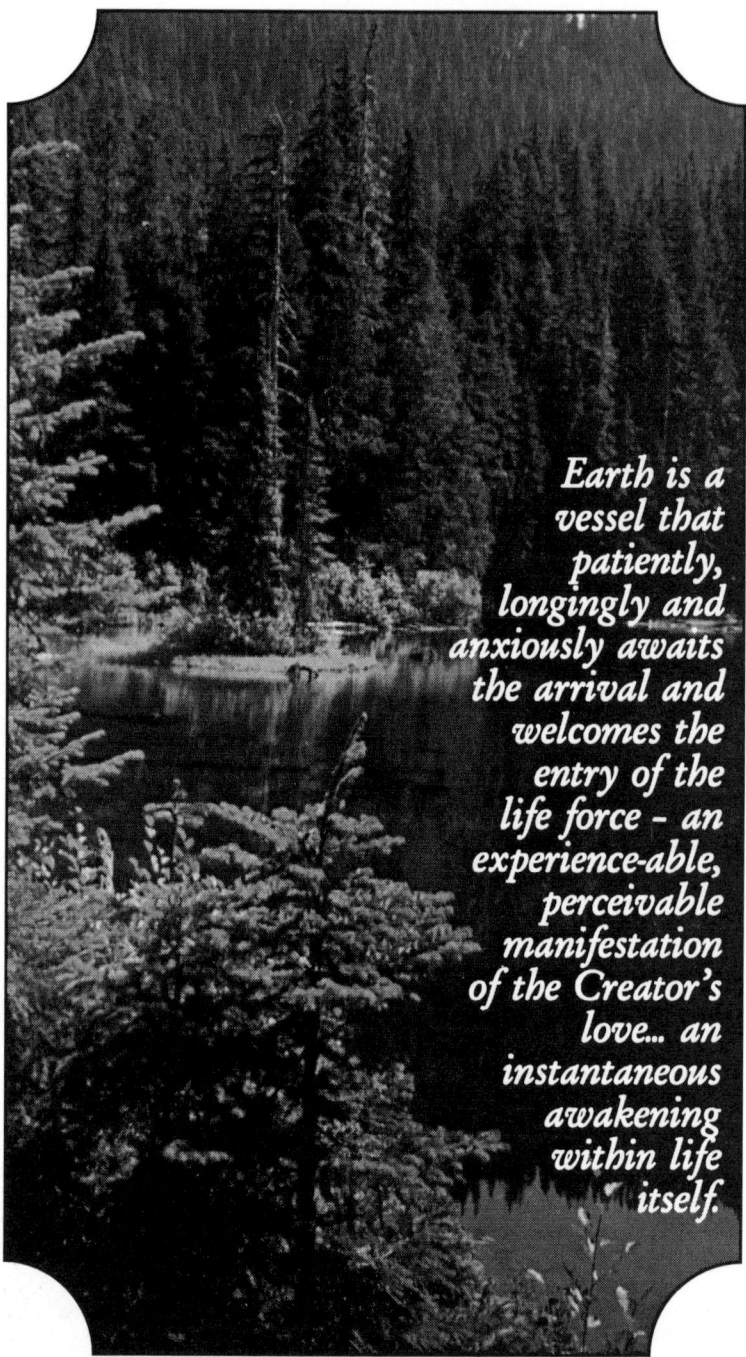

Earth is a vessel that patiently, longingly and anxiously awaits the arrival and welcomes the entry of the life force - an experience-able, perceivable manifestation of the Creator's love... an instantaneous awakening within life itself.

Path of Potential • P.O. Box 4058, Grand Junction, CO 81502 USA

The urge,
the struggle,
the seeking,
and the
pursuing
of the
experiencing
of life, the
discovering
of purpose, the
building of soul,
and the
manifesting
of spirit...
all commence
when the life
force enters.

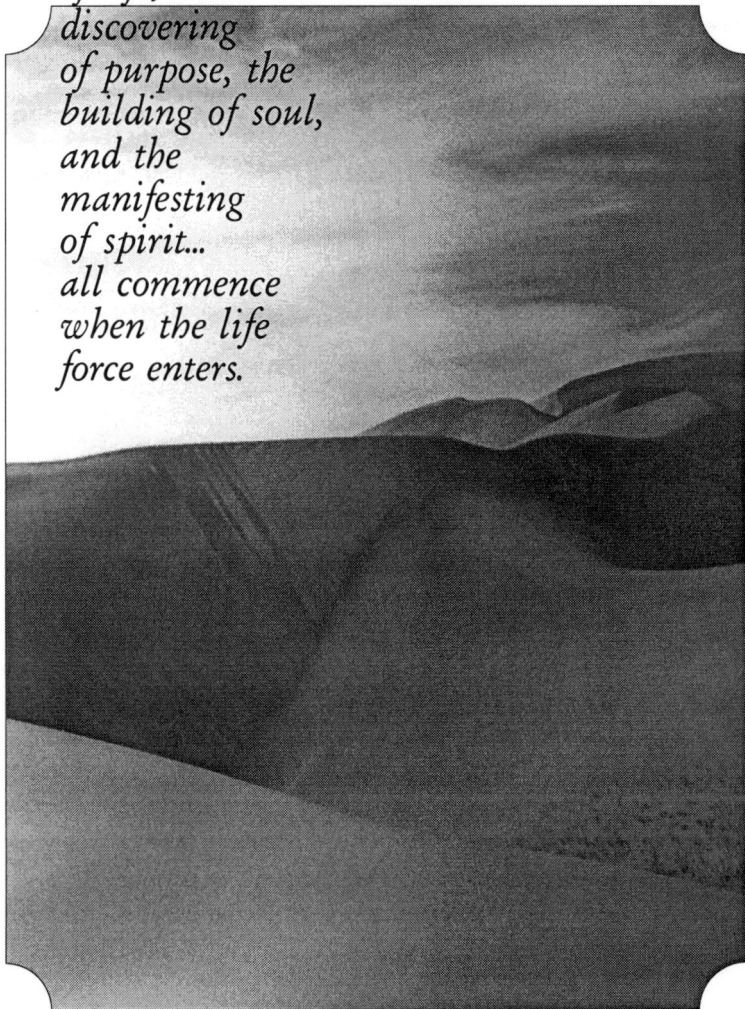

Life puts forth an unceasing effort
to sustain a state of readiness -
a level of alertness and preparedness...

Path of Potential • P.O. Box 4058, Grand Junction, CO 81502 USA

...working to ensure that out of the myriad of life's possible manifestations, life's potential can be made real.

Life,
which holds within
infinite possibilities,
is imbued with and awake
to potential –
the open-ended potential
of each and all.

Path of Potential • P.O. Box 4058, Grand Junction, CO 81502 USA

Striving to become what we are intended to become...

...is a common characteristic of the whole of life.

All of life works to
sustain its
essential
life-generating
processes, to
manifest its
reason for being,
and to fulfill its
purpose and role...
to become that
which is intended.

Path of Potential • P.O. Box 4058, Grand Junction, CO 81502 USA

*Earth -
the receptive
instrument
of the life
force - is the
common mother
of all of life...
all of life
emanates
from and
through the
processes of
earth.*

Path of Potential • P.O. Box 4058, Grand Junction, CO 81502 USA

Humankind is intentionally and purposefully created as a member of earth's life community.

The living nature of earth and humankind's living nature are one and the same. We are unique, yet not separated one from the other...

Path of Potential • P.O. Box 4058, Grand Junction, CO 81502 USA

...unique in role and purpose, yet systemic partners and one in life and its processes.

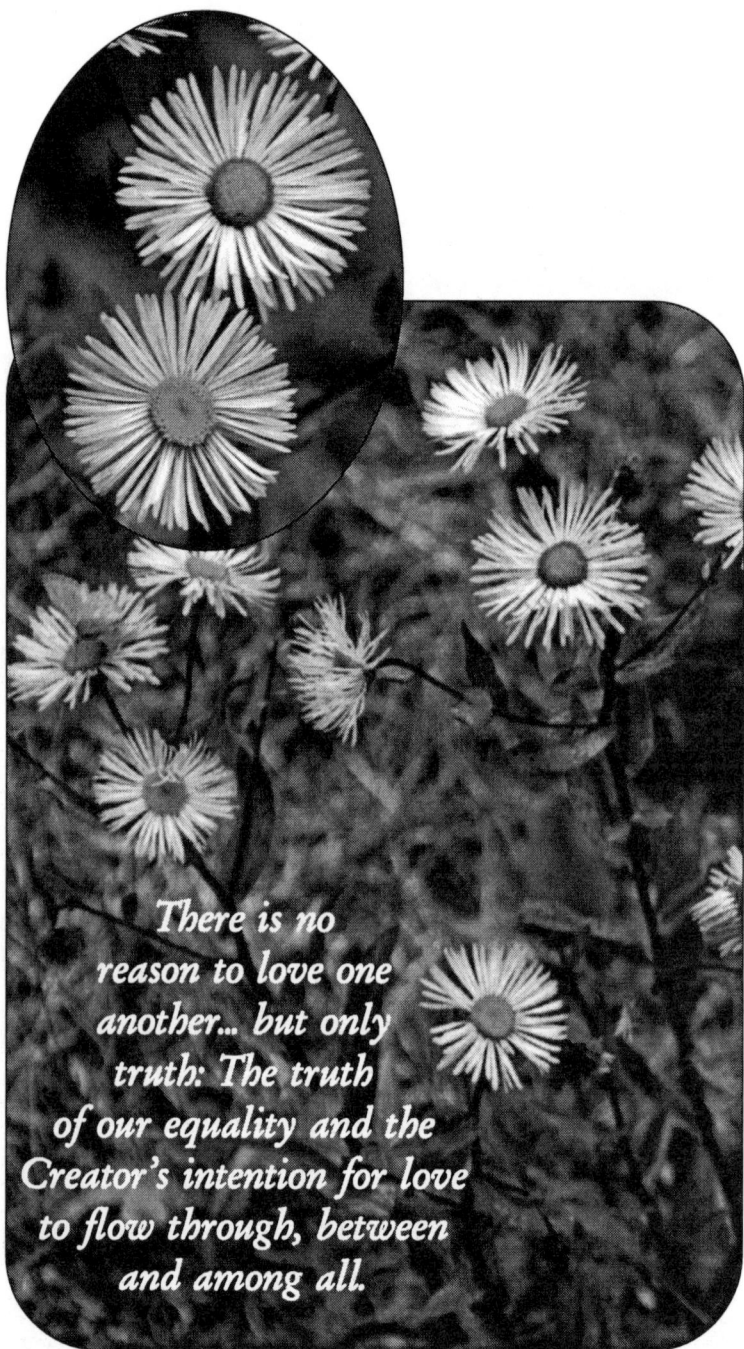

*There is no
reason to love one
another... but only
truth: The truth
of our equality and the
Creator's intention for love
to flow through, between
and among all.*

32

*Love enters
the world
through
virtue.*

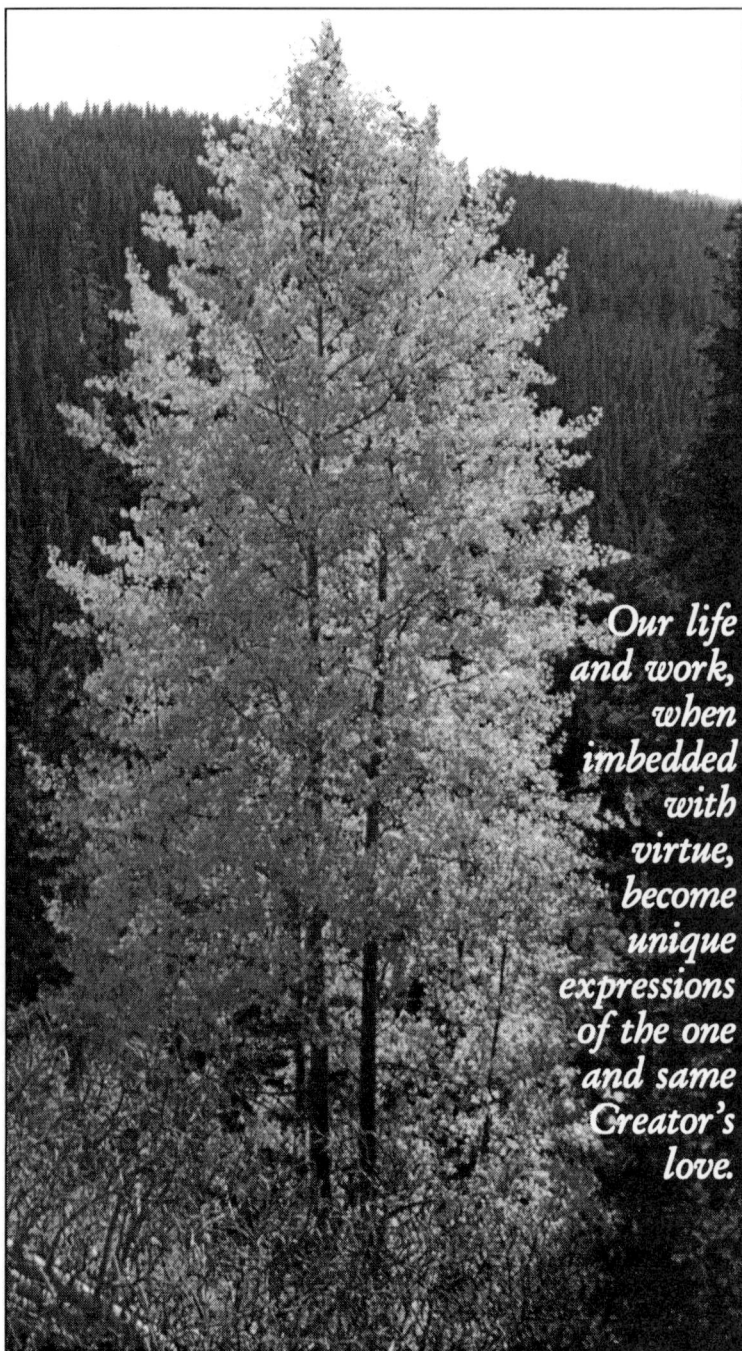

Our life and work, when imbedded with virtue, become unique expressions of the one and same Creator's love.

34

*The ongoingness of life - its path
and its destiny - lies within the
Creator's intention, and is sustained
by the Creator's love.*

*With clarity
equal to revealed words,
the Creator speaks to us -
to each and all of us who will listen -
through the living creation and majestic
works. In this way the Creator's intentions
become known.*

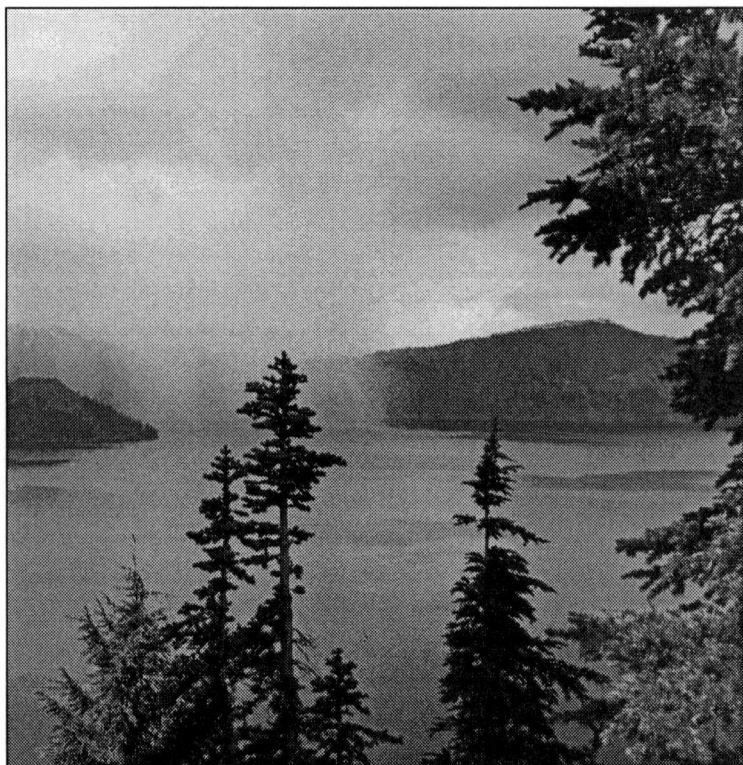

Path of Potential • P.O. Box 4058, Grand Junction, CO 81502 USA

Our
significance
is
realized
through
the
living
out
of
the
Creator's
intention.

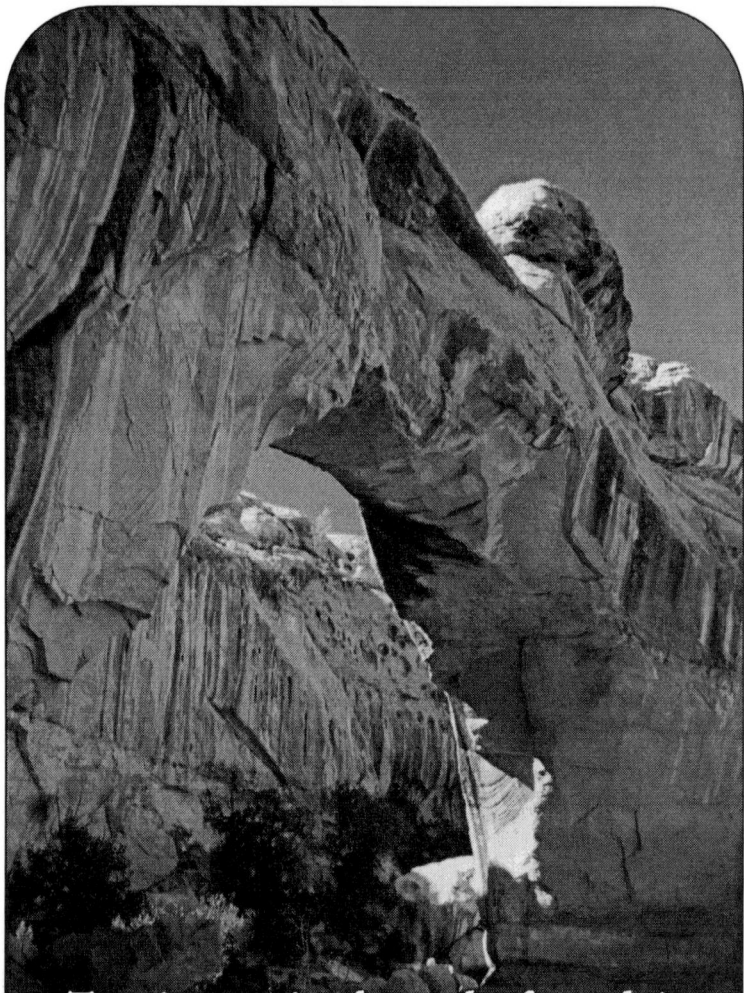

*True joy awaits those who focus their
energy, intellect, and the full power of
their reasoning toward understanding the
intended workings of the earth,
its processes, systems and manifestations...
for they shall hear the voice
of the Creator... and they will experience
the wonder of the Creator's intention.*

Path of Potential • P.O. Box 4058, Grand Junction, CO 81502 USA

Humankind is not separate from,
above or outside the larger whole
of life...

> *a truth that does not diminish*
> *the uniqueness of our design, but*
> *rather increases the significance*
> *of the roles we have been given*
> *and are called upon to play.*

Mother earth's potential is more realizable if the perspective and orientation of humankind emanate from our hearts holding the land as being sacred.

Path of Potential • P.O. Box 4058, Grand Junction, CO 81502 USA

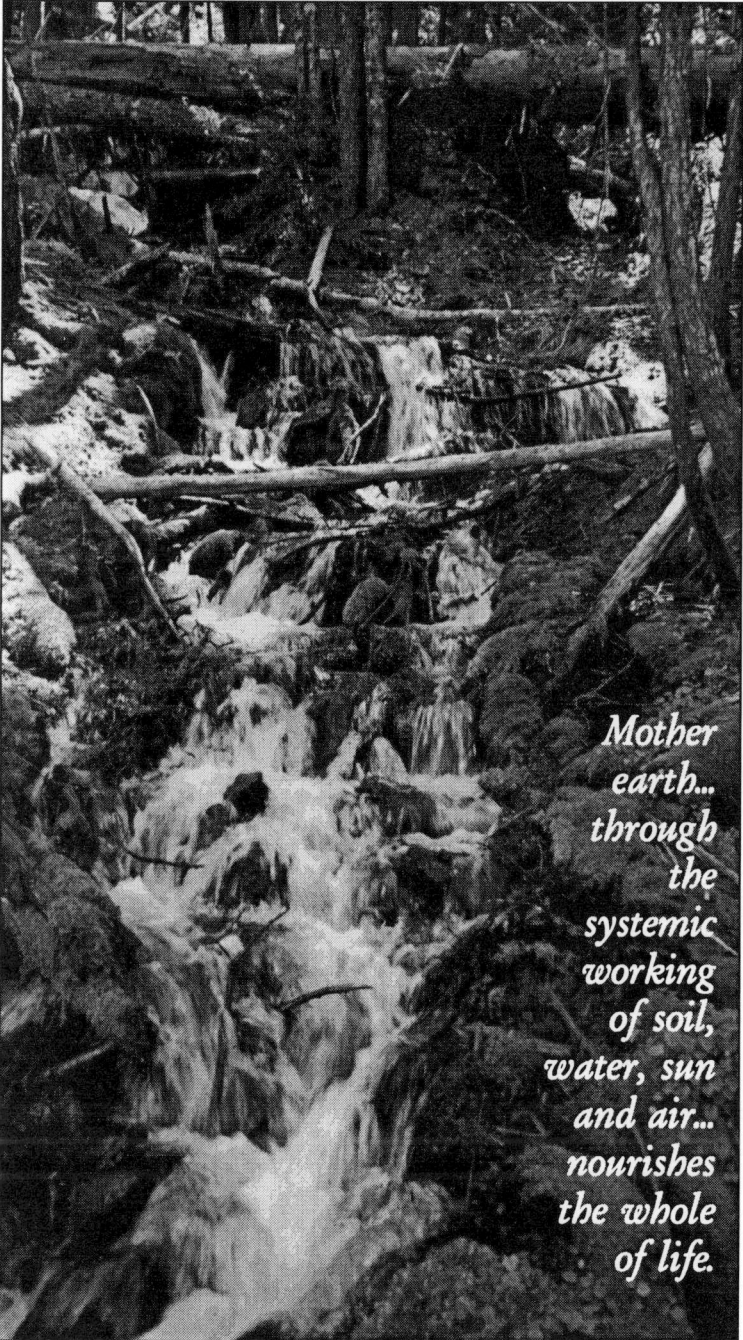

*Mother
earth...
through
the
systemic
working
of soil,
water, sun
and air...
nourishes
the whole
of life.*

A young child looking admiringly at a lizard asks, "Is this part of nature?" Yes, it is part of the creation ...as are we.

Path of Potential • P.O. Box 4058, Grand Junction, CO 81502 USA

The essential nature of life and its way of working is systemic... as such, if we touch one member, we touch them all... thus requiring our seeking, seeing and understanding of the working of the whole.

*Humankind
has an
essential
and
critical
role in the
work and
working of
life on earth.*

Path of Potential • P.O. Box 4058, Grand Junction, CO 81502 USA

*Life, if it is to be
ongoing, requires
sustaining the
vitality and
integrity of its
systems. What is
true for life is
equally true for
earth and for her
members.*

Earth, regardless of the errant ways of her prodigy, toils ceaselessly... never pausing or resting in her efforts to sustain her life-giving, life-nourishing processes.

Path of Potential • P.O. Box 4058, Grand Junction, CO 81502 USA

The regenerative capacity of earth -
her ability to recover, renew and advance -
is truly awesome... yet not infinite.

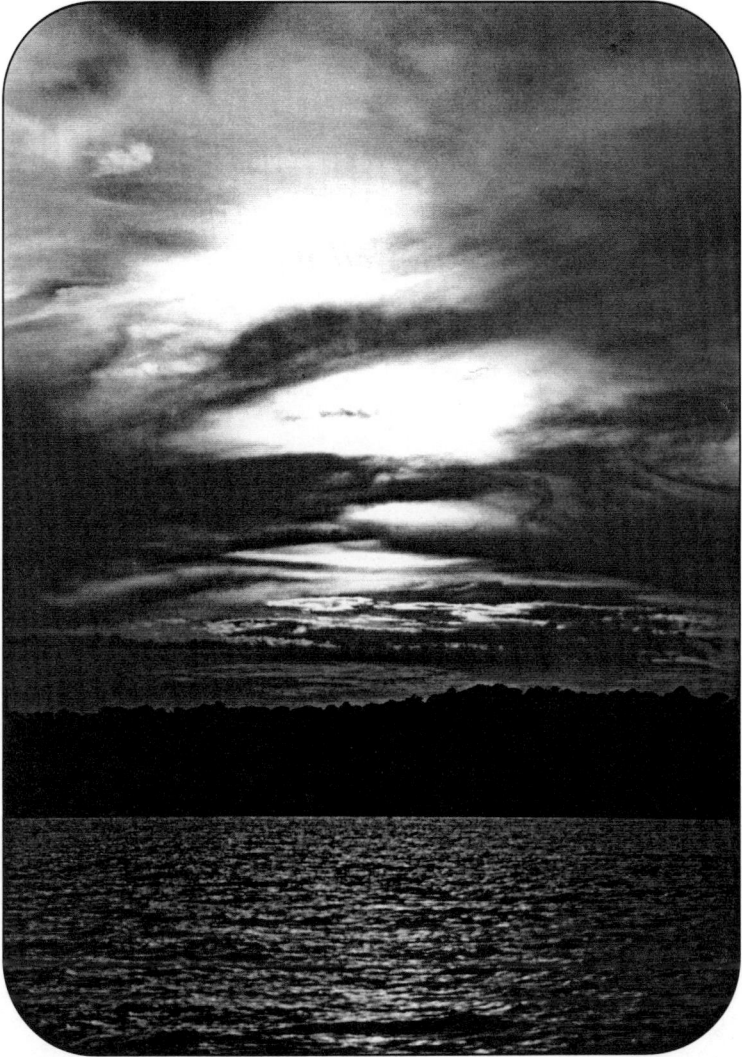

It is possible, in the most real of ways,
for humankind to irreparably interfere.

*Hope for future life of the
whole, and therefore for
ourselves, requires we quiet
our minds to the point of
reflection such that we can
receive the gift of an image
of the good, right and
effective working of the
whole and all its interrelated
and interconnected elements.*

Path of Potential • P.O. Box 4058, Grand Junction, CO 81502 USA

The more we reflect,
the greater potential we have
for accessing wisdom.

A life-of-the-whole-centered philosophy does not diminish humankind or human life, but rather adds significance to the part we are intended to play in the unfolding plan of the Creator... a part that carries with it the requirement that as we engage in our natural tendency to improve our existence – to advance humankind and human life – we do so under the wisdom and guidance of what is right and good for the whole of life... for life itself.

Path of Potential • P.O. Box 4058, Grand Junction, CO 81502 USA

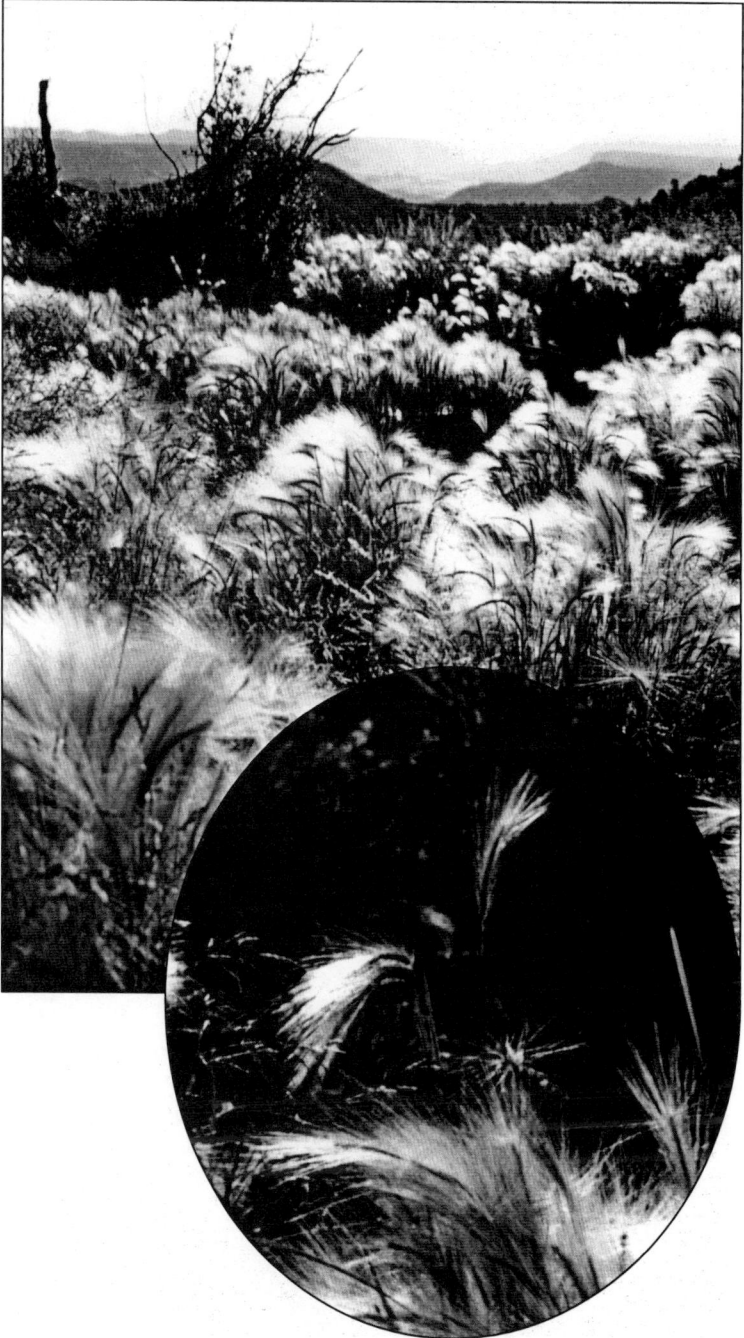

The more access
we have to
wisdom,
the more
able we are
to experience the
sacredness of the
ongoing creation
and the life
processes of
earth...
all of which are
manifestations of
the willful intent
and design of the
Creator of the
universe
of which
we are
a part.

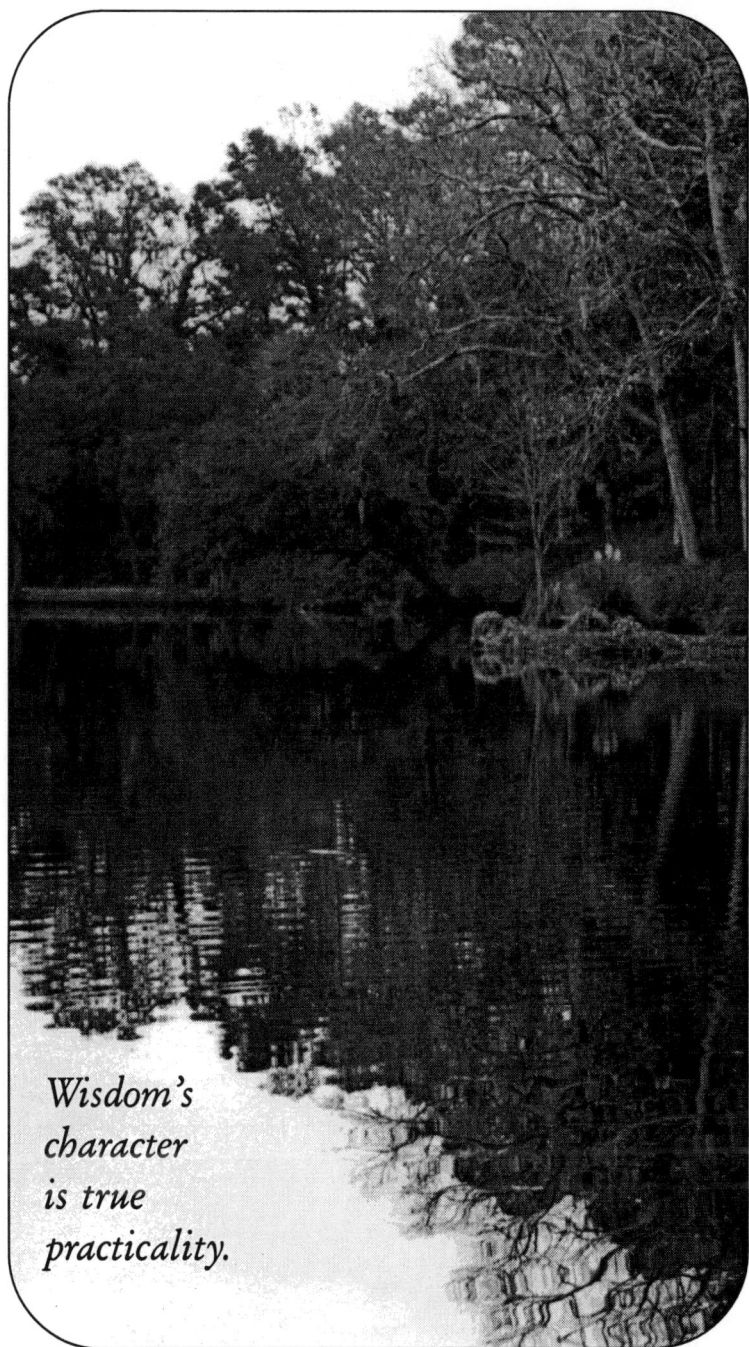

*Wisdom's
character
is true
practicality.*

It is through the development of a "mother's eye" that we become able to see the beauty of the whole of earth's creations - of life's manifestation.

Path of Potential • P.O. Box 4058, Grand Junction, CO 81502 USA

Mother earth's ways
of regenerating her
life-giving processes
- fires, floods, storms, etc.
- are at times frightening and
threatening to life's members...
but inherently essential
to the ongoingness
of life itself.

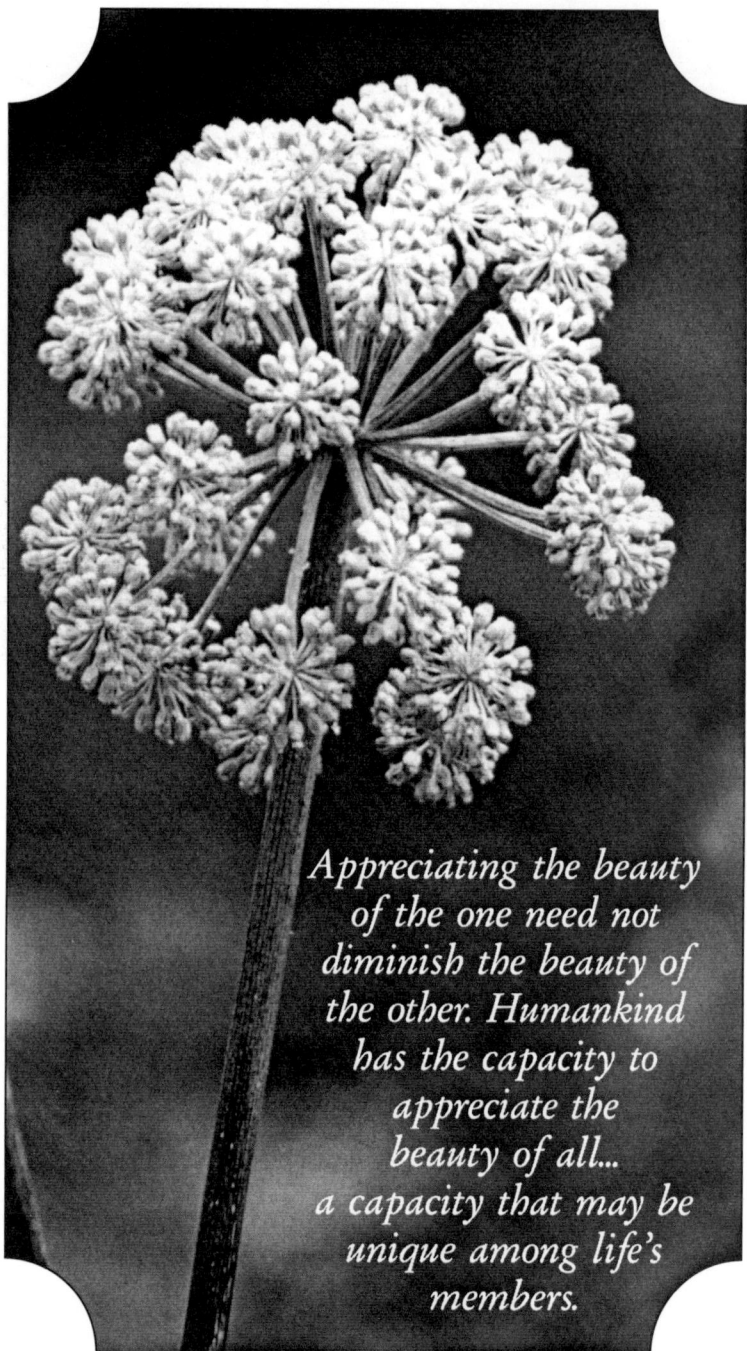

*Appreciating the beauty
of the one need not
diminish the beauty of
the other. Humankind
has the capacity to
appreciate the
beauty of all...
a capacity that may be
unique among life's
members.*

Path of Potential • P.O. Box 4058, Grand Junction, CO 81502 USA

Earth
organizes
for
life.

Path of Potential • P.O. Box 4058, Grand Junction, CO 81502 USA

Honoring life -
all of life,
the whole of life -
begins with
holding sacred
the work
and workings
of our common
mother...
earth.

*Humankind
has a role to
play and work
to accomplish in
the ongoing work
and working
of mother earth.*

60

Roles and work
are the means
by which
we become
that which
we were
designed and
intended to
become.

*Roles
and
work
are the means
by which
we fulfill
our dominion.*

Path of Potential • P.O. Box 4058, Grand Junction, CO 81502 USA

*The essence of humankind's
dominion is making real the
presence of the will of the Creator.*

*Accepting and
embracing our
dominion, we
walk a path that
enables the
essence of each
and all
of life's
members.*

Path of Potential • P.O. Box 4058, Grand Junction, CO 81502 USA

The willful
intention of
the Creator
lies within
essence.

*Mother
earth –
as an aspect
of her
life-giving
work –
organizes
herself in
planetary
energy
fields.
Each
of these
fields has
its own
essential
virtue –
its own
essence
pattern.*

Path of Potential • P.O. Box 4058, Grand Junction, CO 81502 USA

Humankind,
as is
seemingly
true for all
of life,
can tune itself
into the
essential
pattern of
a particular
energy
field.

*Tuning
into and harmonizing
with essence patterns is the
means by which we achieve the
resonance required to realize the
particular virtue - the life-giving spirit
- so intentionally
available within an
energy field.*

   Path of Potential • P.O. Box 4058, Grand Junction, CO 81502 USA

Humankind -
through intuitive wisdom,
the opening of the heart,
and the working of conscience -
can, with ever deepening consciousness
and understanding,
see and experience the essence
of each and all.

Humankind's
role is to enable the
manifestation and the
realization of the
essences of life's
members, systems
and processes.
Our work is to
willfully, purposefully
and soulfully
participate in
manifesting the spirit of
life itself.

Path of Potential • P.O. Box 4058, Grand Junction, CO 81502 USA

Path of Potential • P.O. Box 4058, Grand Junction, CO 81502 USA

Awakening Hearts to Community Potential

*It is possible to live and work in ways
that enable unfolding and realizing the potential
of each and all.*

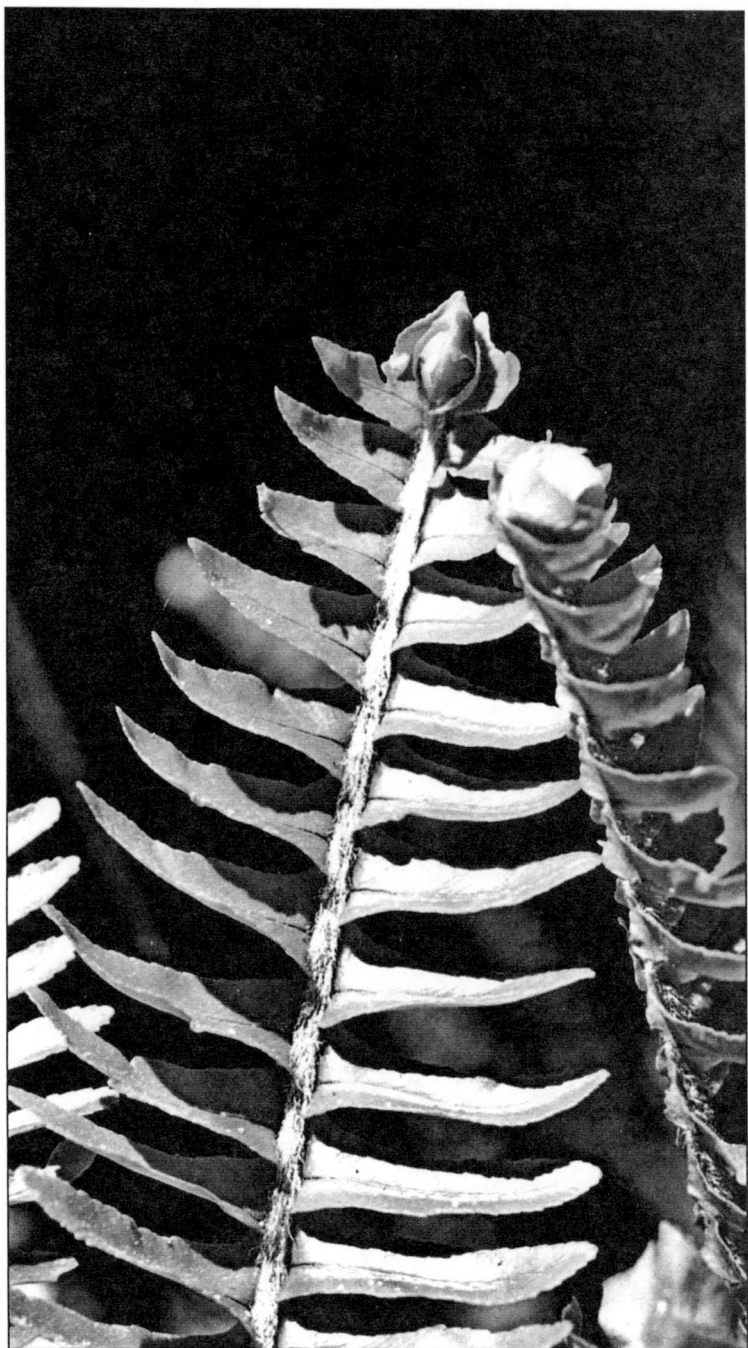

Path of Potential • P.O. Box 4058, Grand Junction, CO 81502 USA

Introduction

A Song of the Many

A whole tapestry... a cacophony of voices... songs and stories of the heart have been lived out and written by many of Kennett Square's citizens. Through their willful diligent efforts, much wisdom has been received, shared and carried out. Each, in their own unique and authentic way, has intentionally struggled to live and work from the perspective of potential. Having Joan Holliday be the songs-person for the whole of the community was a choice for this issue of Path of Potential – a choice that only came about through prayerful reflection and consideration. We know from our experience that the concentrated vocalization, the consciousness-awakening, spirit-lifting song of the one – for example, a particular kind of bird of the deep woods or one of the seemingly quiet desert – awakens our being so that we can hear the joyous sounds and see the unfolding beauty of all that is: songs, stories, and expressive hearts – each in their own way as beautiful and significant as the other. It is from this experience that the concentrated notes and spiritual voice of the one are entered here... one who was there in the beginning; one who continues on the path. And so with faith in our Creator's intent and design, and filled with the hope that Joan's song will find its way into our hearts in ways that better prepare us to seek, to see, and experience the joyous songs of the community and its members, we go forth... and present a sampling of her songs.

The source of all issues facing humanity,
life and earth itself
is the absence of our having realized
our potential.

Path of Potential • P.O. Box 4058, Grand Junction, CO 81502 USA

Can Community Develop Teens' Potential?

It began when I was told my community nursing hours with teen moms would be cut back. Teen pregnancy was increasing while hours available to spend with teen moms were dropping in number. This time of transition caused me to reflect on my thinking which focused primarily on teen pregnancy as an *issue,* and to explore how I would think about teen pregnancy if I began my thinking from *potential.*

It seems our normal way of working in this country is one of identifying issues and then creating a collection of functions to deal with each issue. An example of a collection of functions operating around the teen moms includes health care professionals, tutors, parents, teachers, childcare workers, nutritionists, and welfare workers. Each function usually develops an approach from its own individual perspective of the issue, but rarely works with the other functions to develop an approach as a whole. A consequence of this is that the functions become dependent on the continuation of the issue for their own survival. It is clear to me that we no longer can afford this model; our community does not have the resources required to continue to work this way. For that matter, neither does our country.

To move beyond this dominant model focused on issues and addressed by functions, it would be necessary to work with others to develop thinking that *comes from potential and looks at the whole.* If we began from an image of what is possible for teens in the context of community, we could become agents in teens' development.

I began forming a core team composed of community members (people who were invested in teen development) to develop thinking for a wholistic leadership process. It became necessary for us to orient ourselves to the whole community and to the particular value adding process of which the teen mom was a part. Kennett Square is our whole community. We identified the particular value adding process as family. Teening and parenting are two developmental processes through which family adds value to community; teening builds essential foundational capacities for parenting. With a teen mom, the cycles overlap. Parenting disturbs and perturbs developmental teening; teening disturbs and perturbs developmental parenting.

Our first effort was identifying the work of teening in the context of the value adding process of family as it all relates to a healthy working Kennett Square community. We reflected on the energy we each experienced as a teenager, explored the natural positive energy under the issues that occur with teens, and looked at the essential value of the teen years. We formulated the following as the work of teening:

> To develop the capacity to manage the self that is exploring and experimenting with different energy fields... in a way that he or she progressively develops the capacity for balancing and regulating mental and bodily energies... so that he or she becomes self-determining in what leads their thinking and behavior without creating undue burden to self and society.

I personally shared this work statement with teen moms on routine home visits as well as in groups of teens that I brought together to explore the potential of teening. I was amazed at how quickly they related to it. There was unanimous agreement that

Path of Potential • P.O. Box 4058, Grand Junction, CO 81502 USA

teens wanted "space" to explore and experiment, and also needed and desired different energy fields in community so that they could develop the capacity for balancing their energies.

Several of the teen moms pointed out that their families were strict and did not leave "space" for discussion and questions. Other teens agreed that they were not "thinking" when their exploration went too far, and that ultimately they did not want to "cause problems or issues" for themselves or society. Some teens spoke about the trusting and supportive relationships they had with their grandparents. It seemed their grandparents understood that this unique phase of life had meaning and purpose. Yes, this "work of teening" statement provides a means for all of us to better understand both the intention of the teening years, and how we can support or hinder the teen's development towards becoming self-managing and self-determining.

The core group built upon the understanding we were developing with the teens. It was easy to see that the activity of teening plays an important societal role. Through the work of becoming self-determining, teens discover their uniqueness and build their capacity to bring about a beneficial evolution in societal systems. The essential value of teening is that of developing a personal frame of reference from which to live their lives. Just like the work of lifting weights develops muscle strength, teening works to develop the capacity to see the REALITY of and make REAL all societal processes.

It was at this point that I understood that our current community process did not provide the vitalizing environment for the activity of teening. If the community wished to benefit from these young folks expressing their uniqueness, the community itself would need to shift. Segments of our community were functioning well, but we were missing the community working as a whole with all its interrelated elements to bring "life to its streets."

The core team developed the thinking that is essential for repotentializing community and bringing forth teens' potential. It is obvious that teens are drawn to enlivening energy, so the goal of our community would need to bring dynamism back to interactions. Teens have a built-in capacity for spontaneity and look for arenas to test their development, so our community must promote processes where spontaneity can be expressed. Keeping our youth - the source of our community's future - in mind, we must serve the vision of: *Kennett Square - Every day a better place to grow up in and grow old in.* To activate the shift in our community toward potential, we would need to bring together the "heartfelt energy" in Kennett Square and ask for volunteer involvement from this source.

Our community has come together around a host of heartfelt initiatives focusing on potential. Community processes such as tutoring and mentoring in church basements, pizzerias, and the local library, and creating town festivals and community sings are providing arenas for teens to experiment and explore their potential in a livelier fashion beyond their homes and schools. The whole community is providing arenas for teens to discover who they are and who they can become. Teens are seeing their potential in the community and are beginning to actualize it.

But I am a health nurse! Why would I take on the role of leading a repotentializing community process? And then again, why not me? Instead of asking, "Can it be done," I am saying, "It MUST be done!" I, along with the Kennett Square community, am putting my heartfelt energy into the essential thinking and work.

In essence and in spirit,
we are each unique
and we are all equal.

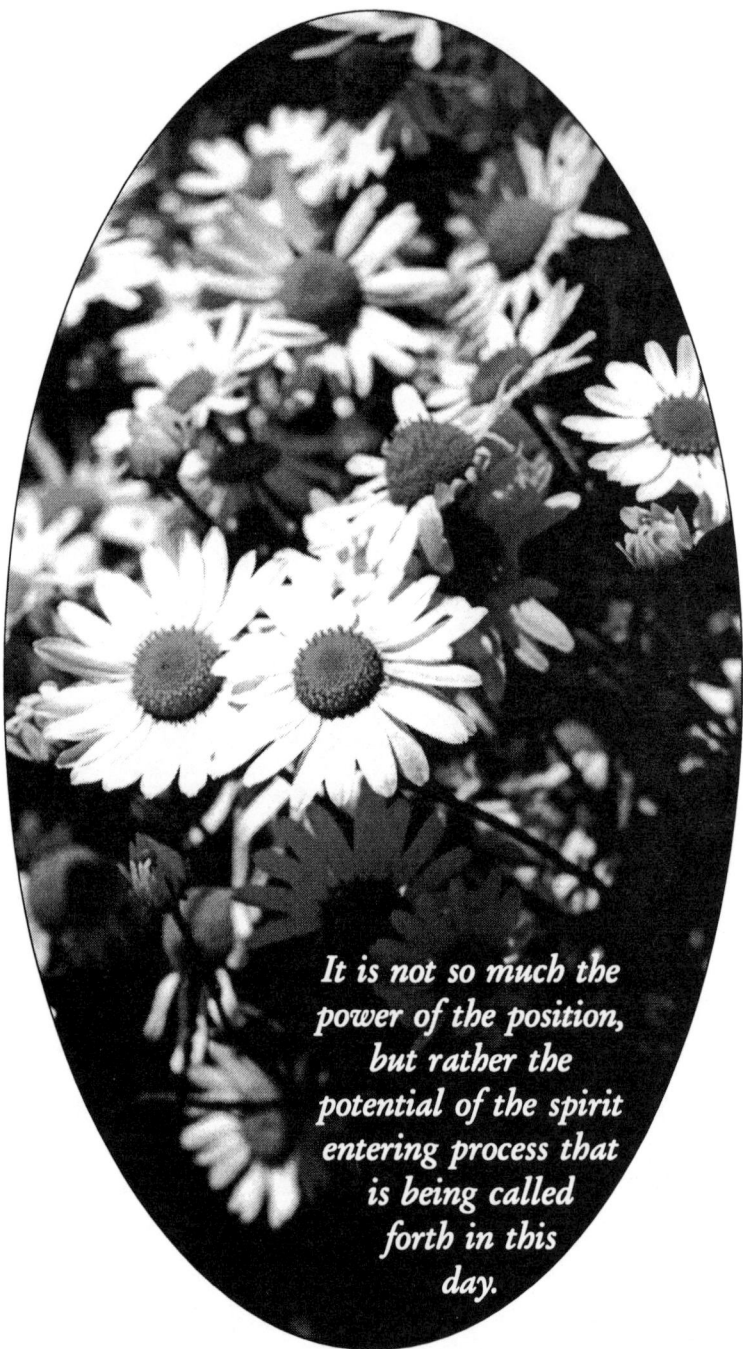

It is not so much the power of the position, but rather the potential of the spirit entering process that is being called forth in this day.

Path of Potential • P.O. Box 4058, Grand Junction, CO 81502 USA

Fall, 1998

Leading a Heartfelt Community Process through Principles

As a long-time community health nurse, my work brought me into all areas of the Kennett Square community and revealed life's broad spectrum. Making home visits, I was many times struck by the lively spirit of the struggling poor as well as by the comfort of the other segments of the community. Although this community is small when compared to our neighboring cities of Philadelphia and Wilmington, the varied "worlds" within Kennett seemed to know very little about each other.

I reflected on the nature of this land and the people who were drawn to this area. First the peaceful Algonquin Indians came, followed by the inclusive Quakers. It is not a surprise these two groups settled here. The "land" is home to one of the greatest variety of flora and fauna anywhere in the country. The core process of *peaceful progressive inclusion* continues today. Could we harmonize with that core process? Could we take it as our living philosophy?

The community is colorful; it holds a diverse representation of life. At the same time, through my community nursing work, I sadly experienced a lack of unity and crossing over of the different cultures, economic groups, and age groups. In essence, I saw that the community had no way to meet in the middle — where human spirit and potential become significant and differences drop away.

We had several small community meetings with participants from all walks of Kennett Square life. We learned about each other and shared and tapped resources. A Listening Project conducted by a local church helped us become more reflective about our community. Creative Grandparenting processes deepened our understanding of the value of "coming from the heart" and joining the two ends of life's spectrum.

My desire to see the community creating a unifying process caused me to become receptive to extending my role beyond community health nursing leadership to leadership required for this synergistic community process. How could a community refuse a group of individuals who led a community effort through bringing together the young and old? In fact, does not everyone relate in some way to the essential vitality and energy of the youth and the wisdom of experience of the older generation? Is this not a facet of life that crosses all cultures and economic groups?

And so, COMMUNITY BRIDGING GENERATIONS was born! We developed an overriding principle: *Community is our lowest common denominator.* We called people together with this as our starting point. We then held up our vision: *Kennett Square - Every day a better place to grow up in and to grow old in.* Most importantly, we saw our work as one of encouraging and supporting ongoing processes of grandparenting, storytelling, mentoring, tutoring, coaching, etc., to help repotentialize and unify the community.

Soon after initiating this good work, I faced many temptations. Entities started attaching to the efforts for their personal agendas. There were offers for funding. Others started engaging the work as a "program" instead of as an ongoing process. The temptation to join these energies was strong. On further reflection, I could see that these offers were real threats to the life-giving heart source from which we had started. At this time, I understood the importance of forming a core group to help develop guiding principles to protect the potential of and provide leadership for our shared vision. Together we are learning to build community leadership processes.

To address the temptation of making COMMUNITY BRIDGING GENERATIONS "a personal agenda," we established the principle: *The overall group belongs to community; thus we will operate as an open free process.* We decided our purpose would be one of providing the arena (community gatherings every six weeks) to share common energy and encourage the processes of grandparenting, tutoring, mentoring, etc., in ever-growing ways. We do not want to be identified with one given effort. On a personal level, we operate by the principle: *Each person is responsible for playing a role that best matches his/her heart-felt energy and builds ongoing community vitality.*

The other side of "the agenda" temptation is one of becoming bogged down by the many issues and problems that any community encounters. When issues come up and individuals express heartfelt concern regarding these issues, we bring the focus to the potential side. What better way to deal with drugs, teen pregnancy, and unemployment than to be involved in an ongoing process of grandparenting, tutoring, and mentoring? Our principle is: *We will focus on and encourage processes that work on potential and positive energy.*

To address the temptation of being viewed as "a program," we hold our meetings at different locations to move about the community and bring in different elements of the community. The principle we follow: *We will keep our community interactions dynamic and all-inclusive.*

The "funding" temptation has also been strong because our efforts that focus on interactions with children also fit into popular funding grants. The following continues to stand and serve as our overall guiding principle: *"Coming from the heart" is free.*

Volunteer support is our free human resource. If funding is pursued, it will be by another entity. COMMUNITY BRIDGING GENERATIONS is pure process. It generates the energy, processes and freedom that are needed to initiate volunteerism. Others may pursue available grant moneys to help support basic start-up costs for initiatives that support potentialization. We see two hazards in accepting traditional funding. One is, conventional funding structures may tempt or require us to serve the funder instead of serving the future potential of the community. Second is the hazard of adding more infrastructural burden to the community, justifying that by our good intentions. The principle we therefore follow is: In our work to repotentialize our community, we will not add infrastructural burden.

With these guiding principles in place, we are realizing outcomes that are "good for one and for ALL." It has been heartwarming to see the outpouring of care that is being expressed in a mentoring effort that is taking place in the elementary schools. A nearby retirement community is generously supplying volunteers for bridging with the schools. This process enriches the lives of the students and the elders, and regenerates the heart energy in our community.

The response by the youth to engage the Senior

Path of Potential • P.O. Box 4058, Grand Junction, CO 81502 USA

Center and share and learn together in community is revitalizing. The "Junior-Senior Prom" that found high-school students and seniors dressed in Prom attire and dancing the waltz is an image captured on a front-page newspaper article that nourished the entire community.

Leading a heartfelt community effort which bridges generations and all aspects of a community seems essential to our future as a community and world. The bridge from the past to the future is expanding in Kennett Square.

SUMMARY, Kennett Square...

LIVING PHILOSOPHY: *Peaceful progressive inclusion.*

VISION: *Kennett Square - Every day a better place to grow up in and to grow old in.*

PRINCIPLES:
- Community is our lowest common denominator.
- The overall group belongs to community; thus we will operate as an open free process.
- Each person is responsible for playing a role that best matches his/her heartfelt energy and builds ongoing community vitality.
- We will focus on and encourage processes that work on potential and positive energy.
- We will keep our community interactions dynamic and all-inclusive.
- "Coming from the heart" is free.
- In our work to repotentialize our community, we will not add infrastructural burden.

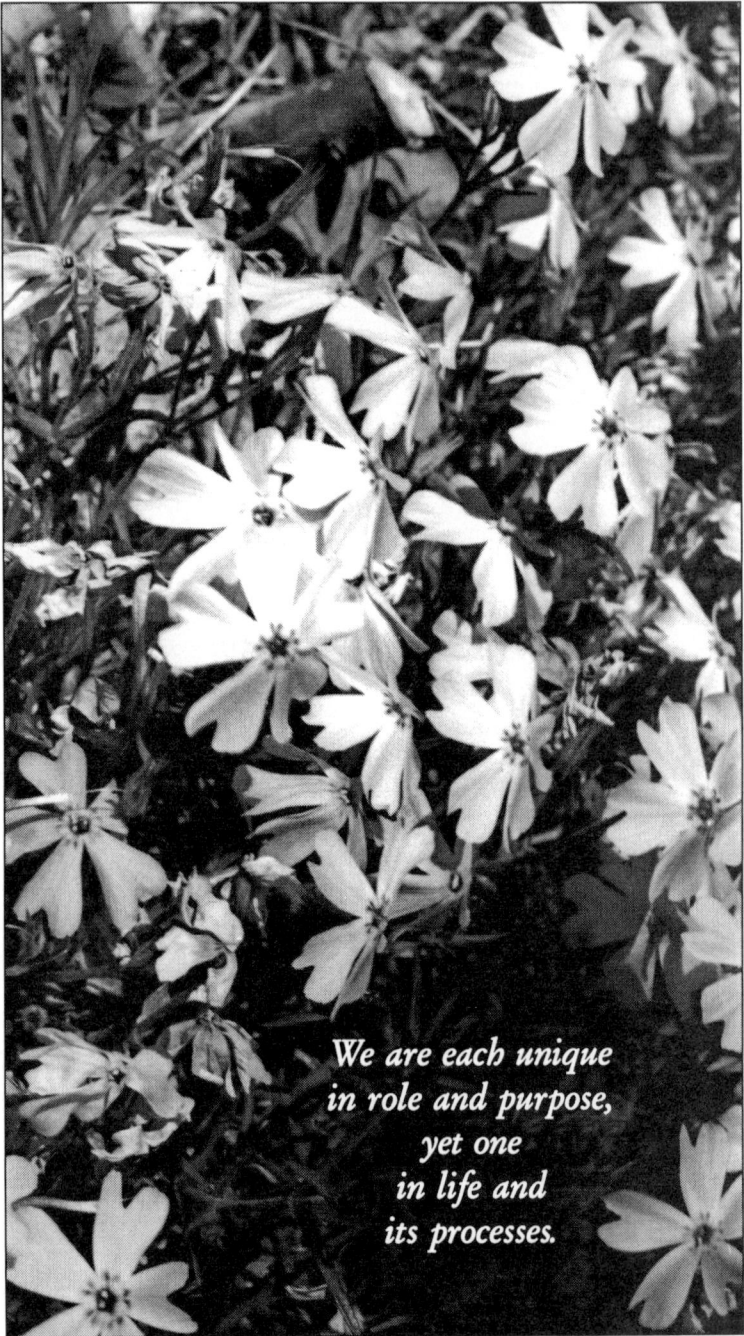

We are each unique
in role and purpose,
yet one
in life and
its processes.

Path of Potential • P.O. Box 4058, Grand Junction, CO 81502 USA

Winter-Fall 1999
Thoughtful Committed Citizens

It has been a few years since a small group of Kennett Square citizens met to engage in reflective dialogue to explore the means for community repotentialization. Our rewarding and significant journey is becoming living testimony of "Never doubt that a small group of thoughtful, committed citizens can change the world. Indeed it is the only thing that ever has" (Margaret Mead). Three key processes have become the cornerstones for our group's work: reflective dialogue, creating a new framework, and staying true to our philosophy.

REFLECTIVE DIALOGUE

In this world of high activity, it has been a major accomplishment to conscientiously take time to engage in reflective dialogue. The art of reflection shared in a dialogue is one of being receptive to seeing the essential energy behind activity – in other words, hearing the music behind the words or seeing the art behind the drawing.

In our Each and All Dialogue Group, which ranges from six to twelve persons, each person comes with a love and deep caring for our community. Our intent is to explore the potential of our community's energy field so that we, each and all, can nourish its repotentialization as we go about our community life.

Our reflective dialogue starts with sharing experiences about our community, and from this we begin to pull out common threads or themes. Always going beyond the facts and details, a reflective dialogue process demands that *each of us enters the dialogue with no personal agendas*. Instead, we bring a willingness to have faith that through this collective reflection, we will receive the deeper understanding of the potential that is essential to our repotentialization work in Kennett Square.

During these regularly scheduled sessions, we are coming to understand that Kennett Square, a town in eastern Pennsylvania, holds an energy field that expresses its essential goodness or core process as *peaceful-progressive-inclusivity*. Kennett Square's ability to both serve as the home for the agricultural mushroom industry while simultaneously support an elder care industry is living proof of this town's openness to the goodness present within its diverse cultural history.

We risk losing our healthy community evolution if we impose incongruent processes on this energy field; unfortunately, this has already been the case in some aspects of our community. With our group's new understanding, we are supporting and initiating processes that best *cooperate with our community's virtue of peaceful-progressive-inclusivity*. This steward leadership of ensuring rightful growth – growth that is in harmony with our essential goodness – is critical to our community's repotentialization.

Through ongoing reflective dialogue, our thoughtful group of citizens is experiencing a renewal of hope and commitment. Through this process, we are also seeing that *we hold the potential to become a vibrant and harmonious community that is a living seed for a world at peace.*

CREATING AND LIVING BY A NEW FRAMEWORK

Our town is waking up! We are experiencing the power of living by a framework that has taken us out of community lethargy and created new involvement and hope. The living framework provides motivation through each and all working together. Best of all, our collective work is advancing the value adding process of the town.

Our Town's Uniqueness: Our group starts from the belief that *each person, culture and aspect of our community has a uniqueness to share.* We believe that through sharing the colorful expressions of our uniqueness, our whole town will flourish. Previously, people's community involvement was defined through job title, program requirement, or economic status. This sadly limited the expression of many people. We are seeing the power of all aspects of the community coming to the table together and developing the open-ended potential of our community. When *each person speaks from the heart* about the volunteer role he or she will take on, it creates a synergistic effect, and more and more people get involved.

Our Town's Integration: It has taken some time to build this new community place of integration, yet the attraction grows with each meeting. More and more of the silent community members are coming forth. On an ongoing basis, we invite individuals and groups to share the volunteer efforts they are generating while promoting bridge building between all. We open the doors to a meeting that has no infrastructure – we only hold up the vision and principles of our new model. *It inspires all of us that we are carrying on with no outside funders;* our real measure of wealth is the energy bank of volunteers working together from which we are gaining high returns. This is the simple economics of the meaningfulness of our integrated work!

Our Town's Value Adding Processes: The primary value adding process of our Kennett community is the mushroom industry. We have recently understood the importance of rallying around a town theme that reflects our collective participation in that value adding process. Our volunteer efforts are now being guided by: "The Miraculous Mushrooming of Care." We also engage in reflective dialogue around Kennett's value adding processes. Recently, significant community issues have come up around our town's mushroom industry. As a small diverse group, we are holding dialogues with the aim of discovering greater value in the mushroom itself, in the industry, and in the community. What if we built a consortium where education, industry and community helped develop a miraculous mushroom? Can mushrooms be used for medicine or as a source of nutrient regeneration of soil? Our previous model was one of problem solving; we now are exploring ways to advance the value adding processes for each and all.

Our Town's Work: Our work has just begun! Mentoring, tutoring, storytelling and coaching have been our first ways of expressing our new way of working. In contrast to a self-serving work model, we are realizing that *each of us is being called* to engage in work that brings about our community's repotentialization. What a lively and meaningful process to be employed!

LIVING OUR TOWN'S PHILOSOPHY

Peaceful-progressive-inclusivity is the living philosophy of our town of Kennett Square. In the time we have spent intentionally working to bring about a repotentialization of our community, we have learned that we need a living philosophy that all community members can put into practice with discipline. It is the higher order influence of a living philosophy that directs our choices and helps us become a vital evolving community.

How does one know what philosophy to take on? Through our reflective dialogue sessions, we have learned the power of matching the energy of our work with the energy of the land. Each land has its unique energy and character. Historically our town has been a peaceful place including and embracing a diversity of cultures (from the Quakers to the Underground Railroad). Our ancestors have been obedient to this power. We have come to understand that we need to become co-creators with our land's energy, taking it on as our living philosophy.

Since we started living by our land's energy, we have been holding bimonthly Bridging the Community meetings at a new community site each time. We developed this open forum for every community member to have the freedom to enter. At each gathering, experiencing a microcosm of our community brings to life what it means to be living *peacefully–progressively-inclusively.* When forty to fifty individuals share the good news of their bridge building efforts aimed at community repotentialization, followed by a process that builds more bridges, our philosophy becomes practical and an ongoing practice. Each ensuing year, the meetings' attendees continue to reflect the next circle of community.

Another example of how we have gained by living to the discipline of our philosophy is demonstrated in a volunteer after-school tutoring process. Three years ago, one community church started with an idea inspired by our philosophy – bringing the vulnerable student into our community circle. The model was shared at Bridging the Community meetings. One church modeling and sharing the spirit about the effort inspired three other churches to develop their unique outreaches. We now have four after-school tutoring processes running every night of the week; Study Buddies has now progressed from an individual church entity into a community process. Community members are crossing over from church to church to volunteer tutor; local businesses are providing snacks as their way of participating in the process.

Today's greatest challenge for living our philosophy of *peaceful-progressive-inclusivity* has been one of bringing the Hispanic migrant worker into our community circle. The workers originally came to the area to support the local mushroom industry, but now are bringing their families to become permanent members of our community. Instead of forcing tolerance and acceptance through activist events, reflection on our philosophy has caused us to go deeper. Our philosophy tells us that *inclusion is much greater than tolerance;* our community has become enriched through learning about and sharing in the essence energies of the Hispanic people – in fact, the family spirit that the Hispanic people embrace has become a strong community contributor to a greater family peace.

Recently we held a community gardening event in a new Hispanic neighborhood: upper middle class women and Hispanic families working together side-by-side creating gardens and landscapes. At this time, we were especially struck by the wisdom of our town's land. Indeed, we all are growing through living its philosophy.

*Our way of working is not one
of hierarchy of position,
but rather one of distinctive roles -
roles required for the process that creates the
void into which spirit enters.*

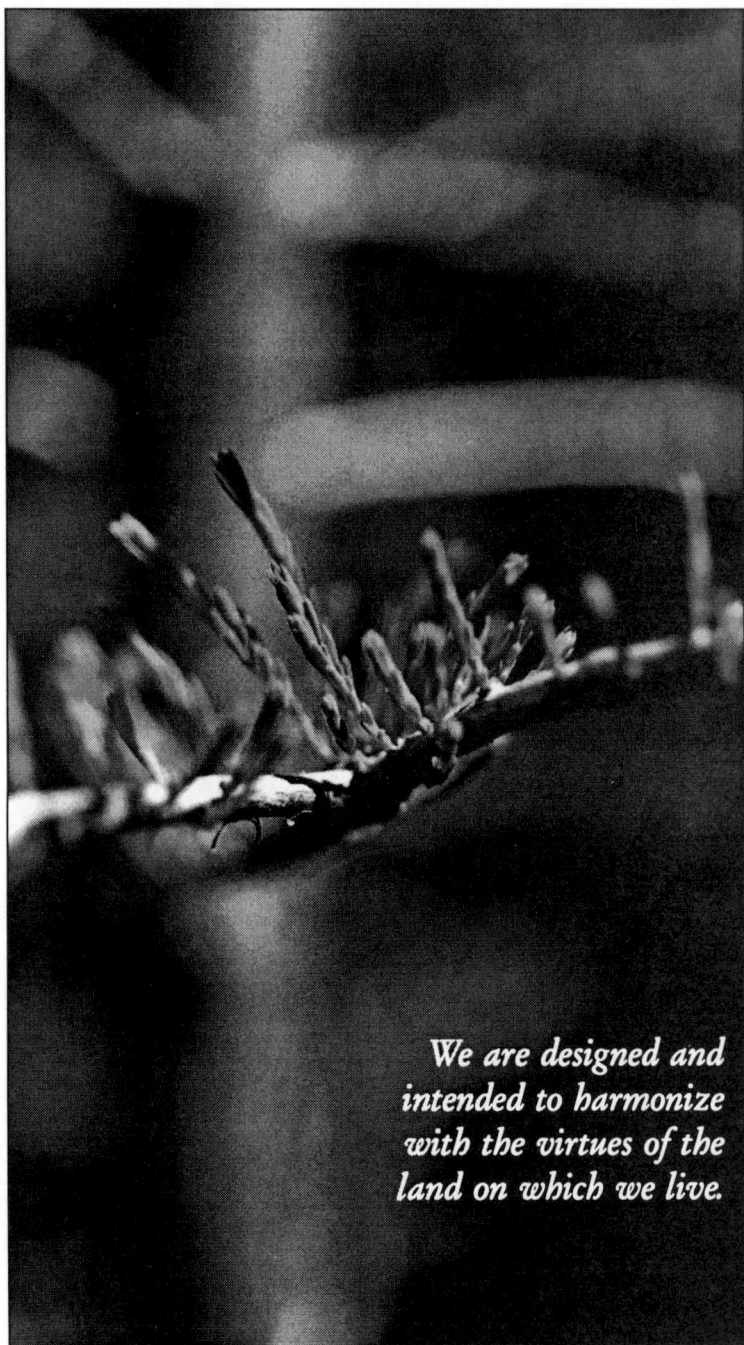

We are designed and
intended to harmonize
with the virtues of the
land on which we live.

Path of Potential • P.O. Box 4058, Grand Junction, CO 81502 USA

Fall 2000

"Bridging Trip" to Mexico Inspires Family Centered Home Community

We were an enthusiastic broad-based community group from Kennett Square, Pennsylvania that made our way to the State of Guanajuato in Mexico. As a public health nurse in the Kennett community, and as a personal volunteer in our grassroots community repotentialization process, I have had the privilege of meeting Mexicans from Guanajuato who have moved to our area to work in the mushroom industry. This trip was my opportunity to experience the homeland of my Mexican friends. Just as importantly, I was hoping that this Mexican trip experience would help highlight ways to bring out and integrate the essential qualities of the Mexican people within our Kennett community, for the people of Kennett Square are working to live from a philosophy of *peaceful progressive inclusivity.*

I found a vibrantly colorful and warm environment as I entered the town of Guanajuato, Mexico; open doors, music playing, and much activity made up the street life. I immediately felt included and encouraged to take part. The vendors approached us with wares for sale; what fun I had with others determining the mutual value to both the buyer and the seller. We also were immediately included in the family fun as the mime pulled several of us into the act taking place in the "jardin" (garden). As we traveled throughout the countryside, we noticed that a garden in the center of each town provided a place where the heartbeat/life-energy of the community could be experienced.

My most profound insight was that families are the single most important unit in the Mexican culture. The businesses are family owned and operated. The entertainment is family oriented, and all saw families enjoying themselves. This seemed to give even the visitor a sense of belonging, and, with the children and teens always near by, a feeling that all was safe and well.

I was able to experience the full spectrum of Mexican living when we all took time out from our hectic business routine to pause and be together. The stores were closed from 2:00 to 4:00 PM while everyone had their main meal and rejoined family and friends for a time of rejuvenation. After the siesta, I experienced the refreshed energy of the business owners who returned to work until mid-evening.

Upon returning to Kennett, I am now appreciating several existing community processes that parallel the above and can be enhanced by keeping in mind the essential qualities of the Mexican people.

This summer, our Kennett community started a farmer's Market in the center of town on Fridays and Saturdays. This event is the beginning of a lively town community process. As a next step, can you see the mime or other forms of entertainment drawing families into the square? Along with this, can you see businesses literally opening their doors to life from the streets with traffic being rerouted to mark the importance of this community process?

As in Mexico, family centered community events are being developed here; some of these are held in Kennett's Anson B. Nixon Park, and others take place

Path of Potential • P.O. Box 4058, Grand Junction, CO 81502 USA

in the center of town. Our town is already called the "Mushroom Capital of the World." What if Kennett Square also became known as the town that "Promotes Family Centered Living"? We have succeeded because of the hard work of family owned businesses. Many have said we never would have survived the hard times without family commitment and families helping families; others have said that the mushroom industry has benefited because the Mexican workers are so family oriented. Regenerating the family spirit matches both our Mexican and Kennett communities.

Many Kennett community members are taking time out of their regular routines to personally volunteer in our community. Every volunteer readily shares that their volunteer efforts rejuvenate their spirits. Just like our Mexican neighbors, would it not be enriching if we made it a community-wide practice of voluntarily spending time together? This would enable us to experience fully a broad spectrum of community life!

It is inspiring to reflect on the melting pot of America and how our greatness as a country is made up of the essential qualities of each diverse people. Our group's trip to Mexico helped us joyfully experience the essential qualities of the Mexican people. Now I see how extending these Mexican qualities will help create a rich, diverse and caring community.

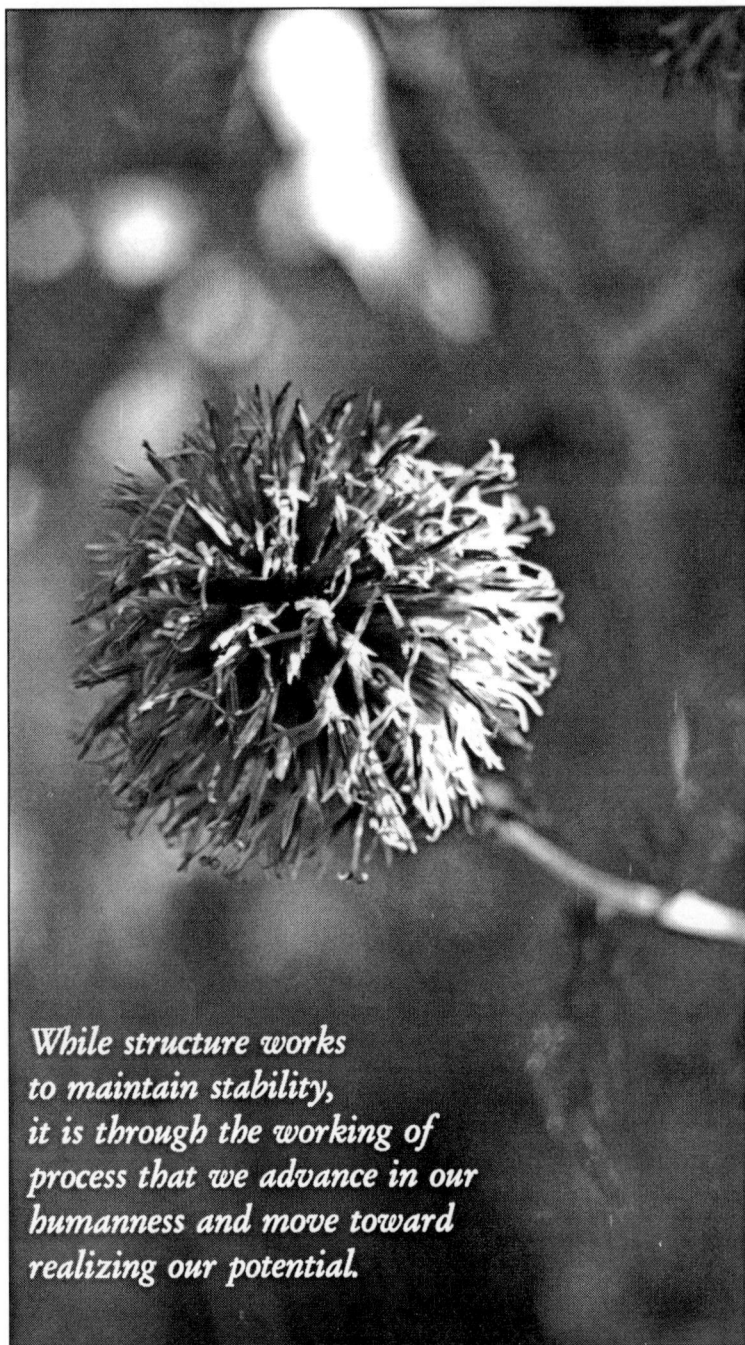

*While structure works
to maintain stability,
it is through the working of
process that we advance in our
humanness and move toward
realizing our potential.*

Path of Potential • P.O. Box 4058, Grand Junction, CO 81502 USA

Spring 2001

Discovering Potential WITHIN the Community Process

"What potential are we going after?" This question has been the starting point for all of my community work in recent years. Instead of thinking my work in community is about helping "troubled people," I am seeing my work as that of initiating processes whereby each community member can become "all he/she can be" within the context of the larger community.

The change of thinking from working on issues to focusing on potential within community creates the basis for sharing a common ground — a place we all share as humans. Focusing on issues creates the basis for separating and segregating, and for giving some people hierarchical power over others to solve the issues.

Erica, a single mother of three, had a difficult time accepting my help as a public health nurse when I was taking the role of "problem solver" and approaching her life issues as my main focus. Since we together moved onto the common ground of discovering potential within the community process, Erica is energetically engaged in community activities. She also is working on her next level of education.

The process has been relatively simple. I moved my work with Erica into an arena that was larger than either of us — the arena of learning in a community setting. We both personally volunteer once a week at Study Buddies where Erica and I join in helping and learning with children of our community as they engage in homework and other subject interests. We together have discovered that learning is a universal process. No matter at what point a person enters the process, the potential for learning is available to all. We stopped focusing on Erica alone, and together became "buddies" in discovering our learning potential. Erica is now proudly announcing, "I'm not thinking about what I can't do; I am thinking about all the things that I can learn;" and I am saying with an even stronger conviction: My best work as a volunteer community leader is initiating processes within the community arena where all can engage thinking and working on the potential side collectively.

Path of Potential • P.O. Box 4058, Grand Junction, CO 81502 USA

Spring 2001

Leading from the Inside Out

As we engage in the process of reflection, we become keenly aware that we limit true understanding of living systems and ourselves if we start with facts and definitions. Instead, in reflection we start with a clean slate, dropping first impressions, assumptions and attitudes in order to ready ourselves for "inner seeing." In this focused and attentive state, we create an open, receptive, inner environment for seeing the energies and spirit being expressed through an entity in the present... as well as through time.

The Each and All Dialogue Group has engaged in this form of reflection process, focusing on the land of Kennett Square. We have collectively seen that our land reflects *peaceful, progressive, inclusivity*. The peaceful history of Kennett has been the result of living in harmony with the land's core process. Being aware of this will now help us be better guardians of our area's socio-eco community.

Our heart and intuition also tell us that our personal ultimate nature goes beyond name and characteristics. Instead, we see that our essential self is expressed through the energy behind our life's expression. Once again, paying attention to our personal core process, we have the opportunity to lead from the inner nature that our Creator so designed... thus becoming co-creators in life's greater design.

As we reflect on our inner yearnings and on our experience of being drawn towards something, or of being "called" throughout our lives, we begin seeing the fingerprint of our personal core process. In other words, we begin seeing the organization of energies in a particular stream and order. With these insights, we move closer to seeing the truth of what is most essential to our individual life's meaning.

This exercise is helped by capturing a phrase that reflects what is being discovered, just as we did with *peaceful, progressive, inclusivity*. In the future, when we are tempted to be pulled into the impulses and energy of others and the environment, we can more effectively stand back and reflect, returning to the focus of the statement of our personal core process and all it represents, and start engaging our environment with the truth of our core energy.

Once we each start practicing leading our lives from the clarity of our personal core process, we have fertile ground to reflect on the core purpose we each and collectively can best serve. Understanding the core purpose to be served causes us to take on a value adding role within a system and/or our community.

We ask, "What is it that I uniquely can give in the most purposeful way? What role will best match both processes?" In this, we look for the connection or "bridging" which will extend each person's core process and help nourish and develop the potential of the system and/or community.

We have been joining together to bring about a Kennett Community repotentialization process. Now we can deepen our heartfelt contributions through each one of us leading from our personal core process, and serving purposes that are core to extending *peaceful, progressive, inclusivity*.

Process is truly working
when it is continuously imbued with love
and begins and ends with dignity.
                    In this way, process is both
                    virtuous and value adding.

Stepping Up To Higher Ground

It is time to take a fresh look at our community repotentialization work and once again ask the question, "What higher ground is calling us?"

In the past four years, we have built a lively community through creating a field of volunteerism and revitalization. Our process of bridging between and among each other in our community has helped us experience the importance of both bringing together all aspects of our community, and living by the philosophy of our land – *peaceful, progressive, inclusivity.*

We now are at a juncture in our community work. If we do not explore the "territory" we need to progressively include as a *whole* community, we risk losing the new potential that has been opened up to us through our efforts. Our vitality must nourish our ongoing viability as a whole community!

From a personal leadership standpoint, this "call to explore" means examining the systems in which we are currently playing roles, and asking, "How do we take our efforts to the next level of potential?" Be our efforts in educating or gardening, we are asking the questions, "Are we caught up in completing a task, or are we helping to develop the mind of learning and gardening and bringing out new life potential? Are we keeping our work as separate projects, or are we tapping all the elements of the system – of the community - as a whole?" Responding to these questions will accomplish two things: first, it will help create the condition for moving to higher ground; and second, it will build a broader base of stakeholders in community repotentialization. Yes, this process requires letting go of our attachments to current patterns, and becoming willing instruments for the next stage of growth.

Our community has an open-to-all Each and All Dialogue Group (which began as a core group) that meets regularly to reflect on our community's essence and potential. Up until now, our group has been a source of inspiration for our community efforts within our individual systems... but we also need to step up and out. We need to come together as *one system* in unified leadership. Wherever we are and whatever process we are engaging, we together must hold one mind and heart with community repotentialization as our "day job." Looking at the area of community potential that is least realized and developing a community-wide process to bring about repotentialization is indeed our challenge. This requires caring about the ALL as much as we care about the EACH.

"Coming from the heart" has been the guiding principle that has inspired our miraculous volunteer efforts. Once again, as we more deeply come to understand and envision what community caring involves, we will have the courage and faith to cross personal and group boundaries necessary to step up to the call... our community's ongoing life is depending on us.

Manifesting and realizing
our potential,
we become fully
and truly human.

Path of Potential • P.O. Box 4058, Grand Junction, CO 81502 USA

"Bridging" Accesses Wholeness

When I was young, I vividly remember when the Mackinaw Bridge was constructed. It was an amazing architectural achievement and one that opened up a whole new world to the lands it connected. The lower and upper portions of the state of Michigan became linked for the first time by the world's largest suspension bridge of five miles long. As my family and I traveled by car from Lower Michigan to the foot of the bridge, I recall experiencing a whole new potential opening up before us; this bridge was providing the freedom to become a united Michigan state. Through time, this experience has become a metaphor for accessing wholeness. Yes, discovering how to bring together all essential elements for becoming a whole enables one to lead on the path of potential.

It always has been important for me to cross over between elements and integrate the whole of my life. For example, my love for and expression of music is carried out in every aspect of my life: home, work, church, etc. The same has been true around my love of family, which has been passed down from my birth family to my own family, and now to the community family. In each case, there has been a continuous stream that has transported and integrated one element into the next evolutionary phase, releasing new potential. On the contrary, whenever I compartmentalize aspects of my life, I find my personal growth becomes limited.

The theme of becoming a united whole has woven a thread throughout my life. With this, I have come to believe that I, as well as others, are called and have a unique design to be leaders and stewards of value adding processes in life. This becomes actualized when one responds to one's calling; in my case, my calling is "to be a leader in the process of repotentializing a whole community."

It has only been recently that I have come to understand the importance of taking on the role of "bridging" to repotentialize and become a whole community. After a period of reflection, where our town's people came to better understand its philosophy of being *peaceful and progressively inclusive,* a group of community members developed a means/process to experience working together: Bridging the Community, a grassroots movement in Kennett Square, PA, has opened up a playing field for everyone to bring themselves into the process of "bridging" their work and efforts within the community.

There are so many levels on which Bridging the Community is adding to our town's potential. On an operational level, we are coming together and sharing resources. This simple and generous act leverages the success of all the "bridging" sides, and in a nutshell makes the success greater and the burden lighter for the overall community. We are currently bringing the community together to envision a "Commons" area where we will create a town physical space for sharing a cross-section of community processes.

On a person-to-person level, "bridging" opens up a place for compassion and seeing heart-to-heart - a place where we share a common humanity. Instead of "walling ourselves off," we see the wisdom of moving towards wholeness. A wonderful example in our community is the "bridging" processes we have initiated and created with our new Mexican neighbors. We now share a Mexican arts and crafts gallery, participate in each other's cultural celebrations, and increasingly appreciate one another's essential natures.

On a systems level, "bridging" is the way that a system can become open and living. Without interconnections and access, does a system not start degenerating? In essence, the "bridging" process that our community and school system have developed is revitalizing the spirit of education and learning for each and all.

Responding to one's personal call and taking on the role of "bridging" WILL access wholeness. Creating a time and space for "bridging" has become not only an effort of mine, but a community's work. Each day, we, in Kennett Square, are discovering the endless potential of "bridging" towards becoming a whole community - a community that is living its vision of becoming a better place in which to grow up and grow old.

All Are Called and
Each Must Choose

In reflecting on what is essential for becoming truly human, having a purpose that adds value to the life around us is key. Within our human design lies a desire to join life's stream and to answer the universal call for making and leaving the world a better place. Conversely, it is not difficult to picture the negative effects in the world when we humans merely extract value and forget the potential of what makes us truly human.

The heart of the good life is having a role to play that is related to a larger purpose. In our Kennett Square repotentialization work, we have a community philosophy that enables us to live our lives purposefully. *Peaceful progressive inclusivity* is the virtue of our land, and becomes the philosophy from which we take our guidance. Lived with faith and purpose, this philosophy can then become a seed for world peace. Slowly but surely, each and all are listening to the call and taking on roles within this community context.

Lou is a retired man who has serious health problems. Some people would label him incapable of contributing to life-generating processes; yet Lou has experienced the community call, and has responded by taking on a role in one of the many after-school tutoring/mentoring processes.

Lou brings his years of self-discipline of being a good student and hard worker into his current role. He quickly challenges, supports and insists that the young student connect with the value of learning. Lou honors the learning that is trying to be manifested. He engages the nature and individuality of the child, as well as his own, as they focus on the subject they are studying together; a dynamic learning process takes place. There are times that Lou leads, and there are times he waits for the initiative of the child. Through all of this, there is commitment to creating new understanding and capacity in both parties.

Lou quickly tells others how this new role has brought meaning and purpose that he never thought possible to his life, especially with his current health condition. Lou would never call his role a "job"; he would insist that a "job" is limited and compelled by external forces. Lou has gone beyond his own bounds and life circumstances to take on a role. He has opened himself to the potential that can be tapped and developed towards becoming truly human.

Because this new role is a direct expression of Lou, he can also authentically share in a church service on Sunday his belief about the importance of taking on a community role. He extends his value adding role by asking others to become involved in the broader community. He exemplifies the idea that working together, side-by-side within the community, is a natural way of advancing inclusivity of all peoples. Indeed, *every person has a role to take on... and every role has equality of dignity.*

Lou is planting vital seeds that have taken root in the Kennett community and beyond. He has heard the call... and he has chosen. Through his role manifestation, his spirit lives on, giving to all of us a living example of what it means to become truly human. Thank you for this eternal gift, Lou.

Process is the means by which we transcend the limitations of structure;

similarly, wisdom is the means by which we transcend the limitations of reason.

Path of Potential • P.O. Box 4058, Grand Junction, CO 81502 USA

Living from Potential
Leaves a Legacy

In the years that we have been intentional about repotentializing our Kennett Square community, we have followed the path of potential. We can now see that each new effort, respectively, has taken on a life all its own, because we have been working from the potential side... not the issue side.

In the beginning phases of our community work, we identified the potential with the people who initially led the heartfelt efforts. It was exciting to experience the uniqueness of each process initiated by an individual or group, while still working in harmony for the community's greater good. We identified the success of the process with the person or group who was in the lead.

So, why then, with individuals moving in and out of the efforts (and in some cases moving away) are the efforts still thriving and growing with new processes "sprouting up"?

In looking behind the life of the community efforts, one can see that all the efforts were started by individuals who stayed true to the community principle of working from potential. With this in place, the person who started a tutoring effort remembered the potential, every child is learn-able. Before setting up volunteer requirements, another individual remembered that each community member has value to contribute. While struggling with neighborhood relationships, a third individual remembered we all hold the potential for planting beautiful gardens together.

Individuals may come and go and, rightfully so, be appreciated for their unique efforts. More importantly, when the individual's heartfelt initiative starts from the principle of working from the potential side, there is a better chance that the effects and spirit being manifested will go beyond the individual... at least this is becoming true in our community!

We each are imbued with open-ended potential.

Path of Potential • P.O. Box 4058, Grand Junction, CO 81502 USA

Fall 2001
Nursing from Essence

When I was in nursing school, a particular experience stands out in memory. In fact, through time, it has become a lesson that has helped me to see the importance of engaging the nursing process from essence.

I was working in an inner city prenatal clinic, and my role was to prepare a first time mother with basic care instructions for a newborn. I carefully went through the formula preparation process, newborn-bathing instructions, and the list of necessary baby items, including a safe crib. My approach was straightforward as I handed out a booklet that repeated the instructions I had just given verbally. Yes, I believed I was practicing nursing!

Weeks later, I was involved in another aspect of my student nursing education: community nursing. As fate would have it, I had the opportunity to visit this same young mother in her home setting with her newborn. As I entered the dark apartment, I experienced a world I had never known before: a one-room apartment with no running water, stove or refrigerator. In a flash, I realized that I had a lot more to learn about nursing.

Through the years, I have come to learn that nursing is a process that is holistic. True nursing takes into account the physical, psychological and spiritual dimensions of the person, and the systems that make up and surround the person. Even though the nursing role is many times activated by a dysfunction, the nursing process keeps in mind the whole context.

Barbara Dossey, the pioneer of holistic nursing, emphasizes, "Holistic nursing is not a specialty in nursing, as I so often hear, but is the essence of nursing."

It is now obvious that as a young nurse, I was approaching my task in a prescriptive fashion. Standing outside the whole, I was the messenger of orders, which I assumed would be followed. This is a classic example of performing a function, but missing the heart and soul of the matter. But now, I am realizing (even more seriously) I missed the opportunity to engage this woman's essence... wherein lies her purest potential. Interacting with her "heart to heart," we could have explored the essence of the parenting process together.

Today, the scenario of the young woman and the dark apartment from my nursing student days still gives me pause for reflection. Going back to that experience, I can recall that after I moved beyond the limitations of the living conditions, I discovered a small cardboard box in the corner of the room... where the baby was peacefully sleeping with the mother lovingly sitting on the floor next to him. This young mother had designed a corner that was made up of what was needed to provide basic care for the newborn. It was then I realized that this young woman understood something that I did not - she understood engaging the parenting process from essence.

As I conceptualize the essence of parenting that the woman of long ago was carrying out with the cardboard box, I go beyond the senses and picture the spirit being manifested; I "see" that this woman was providing a protected space where she had ready access to the baby, and was providing her loving presence in that space. Her parenting essence was

Path of Potential • P.O. Box 4058, Grand Junction, CO 81502 USA

"Bonding with the emerging life processes in order to bring about a harmoniousness."

My nursing role continues to bring me into the lives of young women throughout their nine months of pregnancy. Instead of starting my nursing practice from the field of science, I engage the energy and spirit of the person first. I take time to experience the person behind the view; this gives me a better understanding of how I can introduce healthy practices that harmonize with the essential nature of the person. When we are engaging subjects like parenting, I invite the woman and her partner into the process of exploring with me the essence of parenting. With this as our base, each of us has the opportunity to discover new potential for protecting, nurturing and developing a healthy child.

Nursing from essence takes nursing to another platform. It transforms nursing from the busy doing mode, to "seeing" what it is we are trying to touch. In reality, it simplifies the ever-growing complexity of the medical field, and provides the source from which our holistic understanding begins.

The Value Adding Process of Town Festivals

Town festivals have been around for centuries. Recently, a group of community members have been reflecting on the potential that town festivals can unleash. Beyond the day event, town festivals can become a value adding process. Neither the particular focus of the celebration nor who is at the helm matters, as long as the festival is a reflection of our town's philosophy, adding to the whole of the community through time.

In our town of Kennett Square, we are learning to honor the land's virtue - *peaceful-progressive-inclusivity* - by using it as our philosophy. As we plan our around-the-year street festivals, we engage our best work when we continuously reflect on our town's philosophy. What are the elements that are emerging in our community? Can we progressively include all the essential energies of our town in a peaceful way? How are we carrying the essential elements of our history forward?

The annual Mushroom Festival celebrates the primary industry of our area and manifests the essential elements of a vibrant community. Cooking contests allow our prize and amateur community chefs to develop and contribute their talents. Tours of the mushroom farms evoke appreciation from the town folks for the industry that supports the local economy. Handcrafted items and art pieces from our local area as well as South America inspire the arts and express the spirit of our community. In essence, in experiencing the food, crafts, music and conversation, festival-goers are sharing in a dynamic communing process.

Recently, the Mexican farm workers and families came to the heart of town to host the first Cinco de Mayo festival. The Mexican food, dance and games became central for a day. This first festival for Kennett provided an arena to exemplify our town's philosophy of *peaceful-progressive-inclusivity*.

The youth continue to challenge our community's evolution through town festivals. Each year they set a theme for a Volunteer Festival that envisions the next phase of growth they believe will evolve our community's uniqueness. Two years ago, the theme was "We are Family" - a day of working, playing and praying together. Last year, the theme was "Stitching Our Community" - a day when families and group entities depicted their uniqueness via quilt squares which were later stitched into a community quilt.

The town work continues after the festival. The resources and participants who were engaged during the planning and execution of the festival are now more in tune with a cross-section of the community for ongoing interactions and integration. For example, after recent festivals, the volunteer youth who were once meeting in an insular fashion, are now being brought into several community projects. The art galleries and craft stores are expanding in town. The weekly Farmer's Market reintroduces the food items enjoyed at the festival. In addition, the surrounding communities return to share in common fields of interest.

Our town is making the commitment to add value through town festivals. Living these festival events as one community process, we will learn how to better live our town's philosophy of *peaceful-progressive-inclusivity*. Some say, "Festivals are the face of the community." Our vision for Kennett Square is "*Be the face of the community every day.*"

Path of Potential • P.O. Box 4058, Grand Junction, CO 81502 USA

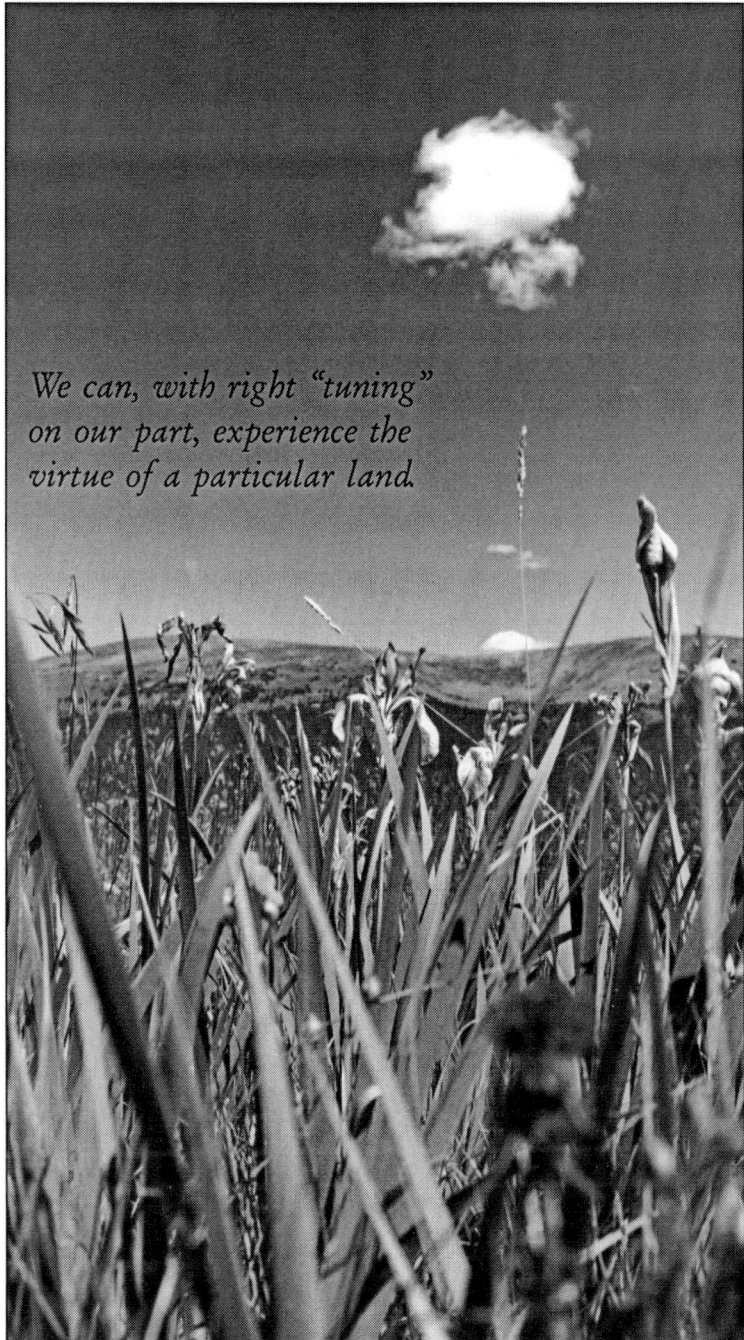

We can, with right "tuning"
on our part, experience the
virtue of a particular land.

Fall 2001

Living the Prayer

Our community is coming to understand its greatest path of potential. We are learning how to harmonize with the essential nature of our area's socio-eco system. In Kennett Square, PA, we "see" the virtue of our socio-eco system as being *"peaceful, progressive, inclusivity."* From this insight, we have developed the living philosophy from which to live.

The philosophy of living from "peaceful, progressive, inclusivity" has become the constant guide for my voluntary leadership role within the community these past five years. In fact, it has become a reflective prayer for me with each new venture that is brought to my attention. As a co-creator with the Great Creator, I pray: "Help me see how to be an instrument of *peaceful, progressive, inclusivity* work as I serve the whole community."

Recently, the mayor and other business folks from our community decided to start a community-sing in the center square of town. The hope was that it could be a uniting and revitalizing community process. Once a month, all community members are being invited to join in a "sing-along" of "oldies but goodies," making it easy with words projected on a screen.

In my normal fashion, I started to tell people about the monthly event and invite them to attend. As I offered my encouragement, I was able to see that those community members who are already active, considered this invitation just another demand on their already full schedules. The fringe community members who were missing a role in the community did not see this as a meaningful role to play. I did not experience peace within others or myself as I presented this opportunity.

In order to access the potential, I was able to see that I would need to take time to listen to the music behind the community to better understand where the *peaceful, progressive, inclusivity* energy matched with this initiative... I would need to stay with my prayer.

After several weeks of living with the prayer question, the light finally went on one afternoon. As I experienced the energy of the elementary school youth in an after-school tutoring program, I realized that this was the group to invite to the community-sing. The children's normal pattern of spending time on the streets at night looking for adventure matched beautifully with the dynamics of a sing-a-long. I offered to walk them over to the site the first month. A whole new event took place! The children's free and creative energy, as well as their talent, brought a whole new vitality to the process. The event grew to include a variety of community participants, and began exuding revitalizing energy. The mayor, who is a music teacher and had held a vision of starting a community youth choir, now has his choir. The parents, who normally stay removed from the community center, started to show up to see their children take on a visible role in the community. Now as official community events come up, the youth are being asked to sing at the events. The hope for the community-sing to become revitalizing is happening.

The lesson for me learned from this experience has been a meaningful one: If I am willing to live in harmony with our community's living philosophy of *peaceful, progressive, inclusivity,* I will experience the joy of working as an instrument with the Creator's design. If I am willing to live my prayer, the path of potential is opened. Indeed, it is not my will... but "Thy Will."

*Reflection and dialogue
are the means of
"seeing" true potential.*

Path of Potential • P.O. Box 4058, Grand Junction, CO 81502 USA

Craftsmanship – an Essential Community Process

As I walk around our small town of Kennett Square, I make note of the tailor, glass blower, baker, mushroom grower, mason, and many other craftsmen. It is obvious how these master craftsmen have developed their crafts over the years, and are engaged in a work that is waning during these times of mass production.

I understand the essentiality of developing craftsmanship in creating a healthy working community. A community willing to pass on its craftsmanship talent continually perfects the craft and creates a developmental process for all engaged. Learning a craft puts a demand on others and us within the community to get better. Craftsmanship is essential to realizing our community vision: *Kennett Square — everyday a better place to grow up in and grow old in.*

INSIGHT: *Learning and mastering a craft is an essential process for healthy human development and for creating a healthy working community.*

Learning the processes leading to mastery of a craft is universal - craftsmanship is truly the basis for the evolution of work, and for the ongoing development of individuals engaging the work. In each stage of development toward mastering a craft, one needs to project into the future an ideal image one is working toward. An art/craft I am working to master is baking. Each level of achieved mastery required my moving through many prerequisite phases - the hierarchical work which ultimately led to my producing a loaf of bread that fit the ideal... that is what evokes "pride in my workmanship."

An individual striving to master a craft looks beyond producing an ideal product as the paramount objective/result of labor, and seeks to identify the personal qualities and character they want to develop through the evolution of their work. As a youth, it seems one learns about their "special gifts" and interests through trying different crafts and discovering the ones which will help him or her further develop these talents and qualities.

We have a good number of elder craftsmen and craftswomen in our community who see the importance of sharing their craft with the youth. Grandparents teach and guide their grandchildren in arts and crafts they have mastered. Also, three times a week after school, middle school students meet with volunteering elders who have a wide range of crafts to share. From creative cooking, weaving, quilting, sewing, woodworking and many more, the halls of the school hum with the challenge, patience and commitment brought out in learning and perfecting a craft. If our elders do not develop craftsmanship capacities in our youth, we may lose craftsmanship forever, as well as lose the means for healthy human development for our next generation.

*A spirit manifested
is available forever
to all -
accessible and capable
of being drawn into
our work and
life processes.*

The process of becoming
is one of being true to one's heart.

Path of Potential • P.O. Box 4058, Grand Junction, CO 81502 USA

Becoming a Community through the Family Process

In our Kennett community repotentialization work, we have taken our guidance from principles. *"Community will be our lowest common denominator"* is one of the key principles. Keeping this principle in mind has helped us think and behave beyond our personal and group agendas. It has kept our eyes focused on the whole community and its interrelated parts, and has led us to see the importance of finding a means for helping all of us join in the process of making this a reality.

As our Kennett community envisions the value of living from this principle, we also see how the family process can teach us the way. In reflecting on the "being" state that makes up a family, one sees the interplay of three elements: *Family starts with "coming from the heart;" family takes on the essential roles for maintaining the family's work; and family regenerates itself.*

In the beginning, the healthy family process originated from the act of "coming from the heart." This source became the seed from which care was extended and continued. In our community work, when our efforts have started from *"coming from the heart,"* the efforts thrive. It also is clear that this heart foundation is what reinforces working together through the hard times. The original energy that starts "from the heart" is the pattern that continues to draw the forces back to its life-giving source.

As we picture a healthy working family process, we also can see the power of roles (father, mother and child are three classic roles). With this view, we can see how *"taking on roles is elemental to an effective working family."* In our community work, where individuals are willing to take on essential roles to maintain the caring efforts that have been started, the efforts continue to thrive. As in the organic family, the roles do not have to be fixed, yet instead should match the talents of the individual and the needs of the whole effort. Roles are also the means for taking on work that we need to "work up to"; in other words, we grow and develop through taking on roles that we are not the best at, yet are necessary to be an effective working family.

The natural evolution of a family is one in which new influences cause the family to go beyond its current form to take on the next platform. This is true both in existence and in spirit. In the realm of existence, an example is the adult child moving on and starting his or her own family. In the realm of spirit, families that keep the spirit of the family process in heart and mind carry that spirit into future work efforts that they pursue beyond their current family. As "grandparents" of the experience, they draw on and uphold the spiritual value of family to help nourish the next generation. The Kennett community continues to move out and change its boundaries as each family effort bridges with other energies and looks at new ways to evolve. Many times, this change causes the effort to change its current form. In other words, with the evolving family, there is a willingness to *"let go of the current state to allow space for the next generation."*

Becoming a community is a dynamic process, and is more easily discovered through working together in smaller groups as "family." Family processes bring us closer to the heart, the roles, and the evolution needed to carry out our work. Can we imbue the spirit of family and learn about the working of family in all of our community work?

Path of Potential • P.O. Box 4058, Grand Junction. CO 81502 USA

We *are* each unique in role and purpose,
yet one in life and its processes.

Winter 2002

Framework for Community Repotentialization

There is a folk tale that tells of the spontaneous generation of community through the initiation of a framework. In this story, a caring townswoman presents the framework. She places a large pot in the center of town and announces that she is making soup to help feed the whole community. As people walk by, they observe that all she has in the pot is a soup bone boiling in water. It quickly becomes obvious that only with the additions and contributions of the community will a nourishing and satisfying soup be created and the potential of the framework be realized. As each townsperson searches inside their heart to find just the right vegetable, condiment, or staple to add to the broth, a nourishing soup starts being created. It is then that "life in the streets" returns and everyone shares in the process of regenerating community potential.

The community repotentialization framework that is being presented in the center of our town starts with the vision: "KENNETT SQUARE: EVERY DAY A BETTER PLACE TO GROW UP IN AND GROW OLD IN." Serving as a source of inspiration and hope, each person is connecting with this community framework that is simmering with and focusing on potential.

There is no set recipe for community repotentialization; each community member is invited to join the open process and to bring their offerings and initiatives to the table. In fact, the process of "SPONTANE-ITY" enhances the blending and mixing of contributions. Young and old, one by one discover that they have something to bring to nourish the Kennett Square community.

"COMING FROM THE HEART" provides the basis for our offerings. This affords the freedom for ALL community members to become involved. Expression of personal talents and interests are all needed and have no hierarchy.

Our goal of "ENLIVENING COMMUNING" is growing. Moving out of our structured jobs and regulated arenas to "life on the streets" is causing all of us to reflect on the power of community interactions and the uniting of energies within one common framework.

Reflect on this framework and you too will understand the role you can play in a community repotentialization process.

Progressively Inspiring New Potential

A set of parents and two of their three children attended a recent Bridging the Community meeting. This was not noteworthy in and of itself, but what did stand out was this family's story about how it has been progressively inspiring new potential through community volunteerism.

Four years ago, the oldest of the three children stepped out of her comfort zone and attended a Bridging the Community meeting in her neighboring area of Kennett Square, PA. She expressed at the meeting that she came with the hope of discovering a place where she could take on a community role and make a difference. The stellar example of community volunteerism that her parents had given her was inspiring the way.

At this meeting, one of the inviting volunteer efforts was the Study Buddies after-school tutoring process; and this young woman's resonating love of children and teaching instantly found her working in this arena. She followed the principle of "coming from the heart" and jumped right into the process.

Throughout her high school years, she faithfully tutored once a week. She found an arena to express her many talents and brought new spirit and meaning not only to her life, but also to the subjects they studied and the lives of the many students she tutored. She will quickly tell you that a whole new world opened up to her through her volunteering, and that this community experience helped clarify the focus of the next phase of her life's journey... a phase centered around education and care for the broader community.

As she moved away from the area to attend college, it appeared to the family and community that there would be a void; when one's mind thinks only in terms of individuals and events, this is a natural assumption. In spite of missing this young woman's strong presence and contributions, the family experienced the importance of their inter-relatedness and the valuable effect each member creates within the family system. They allowed themselves to be inspired by her example, just as she was earlier influenced by her family experience of compassionate caring.

It was not long before the next child in this family signed up to volunteer. He started coming to Bridging the Community meetings and found his niche in the same Study Buddies process that his sister had previously made her community home. Now, two years later, the youngest brother is stepping up to the plate with his own source of enthusiasm, and is bringing his parents to Bridging the Community meetings. This family progression helps the community experience a whole new level of community care.

As I reflect on the power of this story, I see how richly this family is living out our community philosophy of *peaceful, progressive, inclusivity*. Each family member is accessing new potential – theirs and the community's - while continuously receiving and adding value to the circle that reaches far beyond the local. In the world of inspiration, the joy in their faces is the best testimony!

Spring 2002

Bread, Blessed and Shared

As my mother pulled out her huge bread pan, she guided me through the steps of the bread-making process. My mother had been taught the recipe by my grandmother who baked bread for a local store... and my grandmother had learned the recipe from her mother. As she presented each ingredient, which started with yeast and water and progressed to salt, sugar, oil and flour, I experienced myself becoming part of something greater than the bread-making. One of her guiding principles was the idea that the minimum number of loaves made at one time was five. I later learned why this principle held significance.

Bread-making, for me, has become an arena of not only dignifying the natural process of nourishment, but an entry point for value adding work. The significance of the five-loaf recipe became evident early in my experience: the fresh aroma coming from the oven had to be shared! I recall timing the bread coming out of the oven when our three children arrived home from school; this way they could invite a friend or two to join them for a snack. I quickly saw how the "joining together" around the bread was also another way to join together as family and to take the time to engage each other.

It only seemed right to share this natural joy with the neighbors. Many times I would invite them over "while the bread was still warm." It was during this time I discovered that a fresh loaf of bread was a way to reach out to neighbors who were experiencing illnesses and difficulties, or who had recently moved into the neighborhood. The bread was an entry point to freely engage the neighborhood process.

As I moved away to a new community, I brought my bread-making recipe with me. It was not long before I discovered that a fresh loaf of bread was a great offering to present in a staff meeting at my work place; partaking in the bread helped build a camaraderie that was needed for teamwork. It was at this time that I also discovered, at a spiritual level, the significance of making bread and adding value. Starting the Bridging the Community process in our local town became symbolic "breaking bread together." Asking the question, "What role can we each play everyday to make our town a better place to grow up in and grow old in?" is helping us experience the value of working as a whole community. As in making bread, each element has a role; the process of "bridging" enables people within the roles to create relationships that bring new value to our community. Each time we meet is always a fresh and new experience – a time when we energize ourselves with real "food for the soul."

To this day, thirty-five years later, I still experience the miraculous nature of making bread. I am learning that bread-making provides the means for adding value at many levels... before and after our lifetime. In fact, we each may find there is a process that we engage in our lives that we can extend beyond ourselves into the family, neighborhood and community. For now, my new daughter-in-law is stepping up to the bread-making bowl, which not only regenerates our family spirit, but also carries it into a whole new community!

Key Notes for Community Repotentialization

A caring group of Kennett community leaders came together last fall to organize an event with the intention of repotentializing the dream of Martin Luther King on the date of his birth; after all, King's message resonates with our town's living philosophy of *peaceful, progressive, inclusivity.*

The planning was initiated by a volunteer leader who had personally known Martin Luther King. She called together a cross-section of the community to share her heartfelt desire to "wake up" King's dream within our own community.

*"Coming from the heart"
and voluntarily taking on a role to respond
to one's heartfelt call
inspires others to join a community effort.*

The group responded to this valiant intent and started taking our own ownership around the vision. We took the time to read and reflect on King's original message of years ago, enabling us to receive the power and impact of his message today. This reflective process also included our group developing a common aim, which helped everyone's mind and heart join in the same spirit before the work even started.

*In our community work,
sharing a common purpose and aim is
key to bringing forth new potential.*

To help us stay in tune with our aim, one of our community members with musical talent showed up at a meeting with a song he had composed. Being a family man, he merely carried forward a family practice that he frequently engaged - one of singing together and expressing the spirit of the family gathering.

Engaging our work sessions "as a family" deepens our commitments and broadens our community caring.

At our 7:30AM meetings, one could hear a wide range of voices singing the lyrics, "We have a dream of peace and harmony for everyone, everywhere. And we will work for peace and harmony 'til everyone this dream will share."

This remembering process became instrumental to our group's harmony as we discussed our plans and had differing opinions.

Remembering our aim through music accesses a unitive spirit.

On the day of the "Breaking Bread Together Breakfast" – our community's celebration of Martin Luther King's vision - the music once again brought forth the spirit of the dream. A rainbow of children from town neighborhoods worked out a special rhythm dance for the song, and the newly formed community choir sang loud and clear King's repotentialized message. The broader community was newly remembering the true reason for our gathering, and joined the refrain with unitive gusto.

Our sustaining community aim: "Become a seed for world peace."

Summer 2002

Teens Developing Community Potential

Teening is becoming a vital life process in our work to repotentialize our community. It was not long ago, however, that we were addressing the teen years as "difficult" and "problematic." We were missing the true potential in this phase of human life. When we finally got to the heart of what teening is about, we were able to see that "teens trying to develop themselves through exploration and experimentation" is exactly what our community needs to continue advancing its next "edge."

For a period of time now, I have taken on the role of challenging our youth to "be" what is core to them – experimentation and exploration – as they lead a community process that will "wake up the town." In group dialogues, I provide the context by telling them that their teen years are in between the current paradigm and the paradigm that their generation will be creating for the future; this is their time to reflect on the living philosophy – _peaceful, progressive, inclusivity_ - of our Kennett land and play a role in repotentializing our community. They can observe how this philosophy is currently being lived out in our community, assess what is missing to match our land's energy, and look ahead to what would make a difference.

The process of waiting for responses and staying with the ideas that spring forth as a result of the previously stated challenge is truly one of being in the midst of a new creation. Initially, it seems to take the teens some time to "think out of the box;" they have responses that sound something like the voice of their parent or teacher. With continual challenges such as "What would be different about this idea?" or "Do you think you would be 'leading an edge' with this one?"... the magic starts happening. Each year, there is a new group of teens - a fresh slate – with a new potential to bring to life. Each year, as I hold my arms out to illustrate the whole community as their focus, I am in total appreciation of how the teening process adds to our community life.

A few years ago, the teens saw power in creating a family theme by which our community could live. They developed a series of processes that brought about community reflection on family: They wrote articles for the local paper, organized a family prayer walk about town, provided family entertainment on the streets, and worked together to clean up the town. The teens' understanding that all people need "family" and that this is a community structure that is all-inclusive no matter who the person may be, is opening the community's eyes to our next phase of community development work.

The activity of teening is making a difference in our community. Instead of holding back the experimentation of the teen years, or putting external controls to protect our teens, we are challenging them to be leaders in our community. With this switch, the teens are free to develop the capacities they need for adulthood, and the community accesses one of its prize resources. I would call this a win-win situation for all.

Love enters the world through virtue.

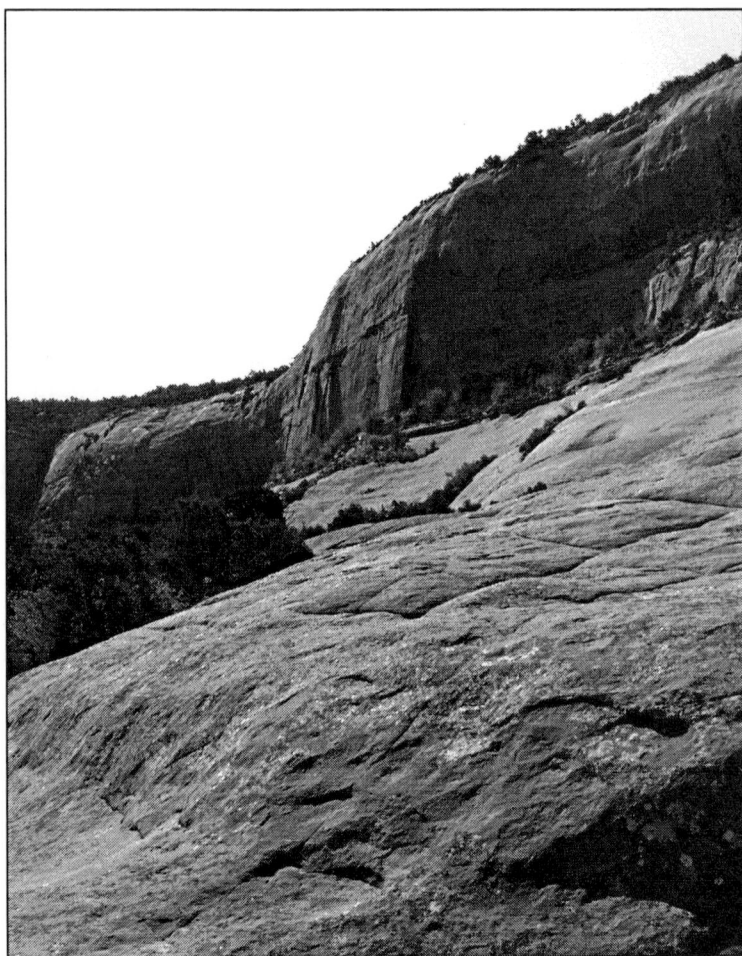

Path of Potential • P.O. Box 4058, Grand Junction, CO 81502 USA

A Soup Kitchen or a Community Meal?

In a recent community dialogue, the concern about "feeding the hungry" was explored. What if we moved beyond addressing the needs of "the hungry" as a community issue, to one of generating community potential? Taking such a communal approach would certainly move us from our current hierarchical model whereby the "haves" feed the "have-nots."

To help us confront this current model, we asked ourselves: "What have we in common with the hungry? What is the whole of which we are ALL a part?" When we explored hunger from this perspective, it became surprisingly obvious that each member of our community needed to be nourished. Yes, this was a good place to begin; we all share the need for nourishment. This starting point led to the realization that community issues will never be solved by focusing on the issue itself – solutions to communal problems are found in creating a larger process in which everyone experiences the value that is being actualized.

Keeping these principles in mind, we went about creating an initiative which would provide community members the opportunity to experience "the hungry being fed" within the context of the whole community. We approached the local high-school cooking class to share our idea. Would some students be interested in preparing a meal for our "Bridging the Community" meeting that would be held at the homeless shelter in town? With new intention and spirit, would the youth like to play an instrumental role in bringing the community together around nourishing the whole of the community?

Two students quickly responded to the challenge and started identifying the phases of the value adding process they would be leading. For starters, they solicited food from the local grocery stores. This time, they weren't asking for funds for operating a soup kitchen; they were asking for the investment in creating a community meal that each and all would enjoy. The menu planning intentionally highlighted a mushroom dish in honor of the mushroom agricultural industry; after all, our community was being sustained and nourished by this industry's work. The students introduced the added dimension of entering the homeless shelter's kitchen and working with the residents to prepare the meal, which became the means that helped to bring all of the essential "parts" into the whole of the preparation phase. As a variety of individuals from all walks of life responded to the open invitation to join in a community meal at the homeless shelter, the event was well on its way.

The experience was profound. More than sixty community members sat at the "table of plenty" on a warm evening in May. There was no singling out of one person's hunger - no division between classes. It was simply a community meal where everyone shared their hunger and was nourished.

Today we still hold the image of the community meal we shared. Beyond the meal, we now have "food" for future community work. Our hope is to have this initiative serve as an inspiration for creating an ongoing process for feeding the hungry within our community. What better way to repotentialize a community than to bring each and all into the whole of the nourishing process!

Fall 2002

The Study Buddies Seed

Little did we imagine a few years ago, when the first Study Buddies after-school tutoring effort was seeded, the potential that would be realized in our town of Kennett Square. Some people ask, "How can this be - still vital and growing since 1997? How can this be - without any formal programming, funding or structure?" The Study Buddies story is one of moving beyond the current way of after-school programming to one of building a strong community.

Instead of beginning this effort focusing on the problem-side, Study Buddies started from the belief that *every child has potential and has the capacity to learn.* With this, a small group of individuals initiated the first Study Buddies, and then the next three progressively followed. The groups did not start by looking for funding or a tested program for after-school tutoring, but instead they trusted that committed caring and a grassroots spirit would be the energy to carry the effort forward. *"Starting from potential"* and *"Coming from the heart"* were the principles that first guided them.

We now have five Study Buddies efforts in the small town of Kennett Square. Kennett Presbyterian Church opens its doors on Monday evenings, 2nd Baptist Church on Tuesday evenings, Bethel Church on Wednesday afternoons, Greater Works Ministries on Thursday evenings, and Kennett Presbyterian Church on Friday evenings for a shared "buddies" meal. The groups have come to appreciate that each effort is unique to its own setting; however, there is strength in being a united "Study Buddies of Kennett Square." The volunteer group leaders meet periodically to plan joint picnics and field trips, and best of all, to share prized stories and experiences. This new mind and way of being is one of moving beyond individual turf towards joining the spirit of a whole town community.

Picture any day of the school week, and you will find one of four churches opening its doors to students, piling in from the neighborhood. At the same time, see the cars pulling up with tutors ranging from high-school students to elders, arriving from neighborhoods, some even outside of Kennett. It does not take long for the "buddies" to settle down to study, engage in an art project, or get involved in a shared game. The energy is high and each student and tutor seems to be going beyond duty to receive the rich nourishment that is a part of this community work effort.

It is no wonder that whenever someone is inquiring about how and where he or she can reach a cross-section of the community, you hear the response, "How about coming to Study Buddies?" Health fairs, clothing drives, festival planning and preparation, community meals, community singing, and scouting leadership efforts have all been naturally shared in this open and caring arena. Study Buddies has moved beyond the concept of being a "tutoring program" to one of becoming a community.

As any good seeding, this community process has spread. In our neighboring town of Avondale, two Study Buddies efforts have sprouted recently. These two groups will have their own character and nature, and yet this next generation of Study Buddies will extend the Kennett way. They have revealed that they will start from the principle of "coming from the heart," and voluntarily create a natural community space to welcome all aspects of the community to work together for our future: the children.

Is this story starting to sound like the one of the mustard seed?

*Our
significance
is realized
through the
living out
of our inner
essence.*

Path of Potential • P.O. Box 4058, Grand Junction, CO 81502 USA

Mushrooming of Miracles

In our community of Kennett Square, we strive to align our ways of living, working and being in harmony with the essence of the land on which we live, and to take this essence as a living philosophy of our town. With our essence – *peaceful, progressive, inclusivity* – as our essential guide, along with key principles, spirit enters and the "mushrooming of miracles" begins to happen.

Each "miracle" stems from an area of community concern, such as teen pregnancy, neighborhood decline, students performing poorly in school, or the assimilation of the Mexican migrant farm worker and families into the community. The process always begins with reflection; then, in a miraculous sort of way, a heartfelt effort is initiated by an individual or group who is strongly connected with the area of concern and willing to start an effort from the "whole" of the community.

To address teen pregnancy, those who enjoy working with youth reflected on the essence of a teen, which is about looking for arenas to explore and experiment. It became obvious that community processes needed to be initiated which would capture this potential. Starting from this essential energy, the community now regularly invites teens to step into town and lead town festivals with themes that advance the town's living philosophy. The youth have formed a youth town council and are voices in the decision-making of the town's evolution. The youth are coming out in large numbers to volunteer at after-school tutoring programs. All of these involvements are capturing the essential energy of the teens. With more options for the teens' expanded expression within our community, the rate of teen pregnancy has decreased.

In the neighborhood decline arena, those who enjoy gardening and home repair reflected on the essence of a neighborhood, which is about sharing living surroundings and processes. It became obvious that a joint process to be shared, such as gardening and neighborhood home repair, would evoke the involvement of the whole and activate the sense of caring and pride in the neighborhood. With the assistance and investment of the broader community in this effort, neighborhoods are improving in condition and spirit.

In the area of students failing academically, those who were connected with the youth reflected on the potential of the youth and started from the place that "every child is learn-able." Volunteer after-school programs started sprouting across town, and now each night of the week there is a "Study Buddies" effort that is living proof that every child can learn and enjoy the process of studying with a buddy.

In the arena of assimilating the Mexican migrant farm workers and families into our community, those who were inspired by the pioneering essence of these newcomers started an Intercambio English/Spanish language exchange. This approach has no teachers and is led by the spirit of caring and the desire to communicate with each other. This group has become a dynamic living example of community-making and the living philosophy of *peaceful, progressive, inclusivity.*

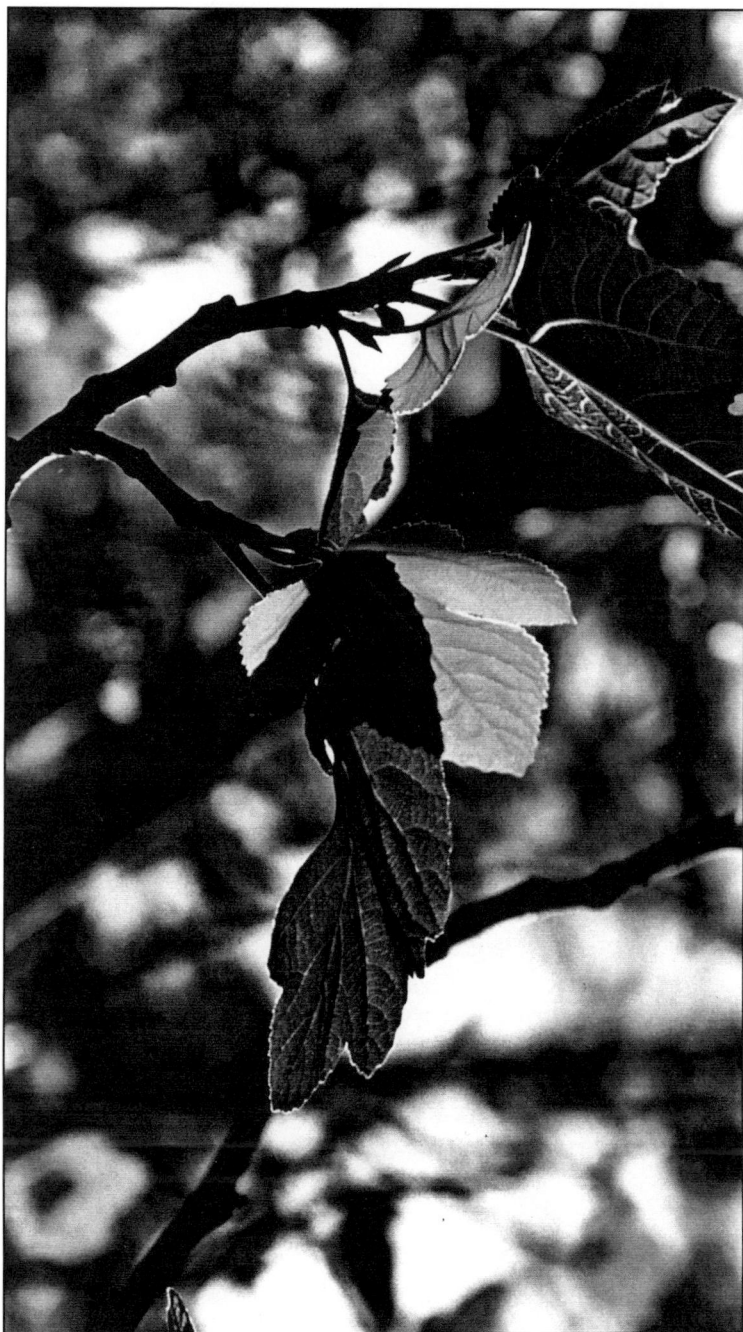

Engaging Youth in a Living Philosophy

For years, I have experienced a particular calling to work with the teen youth in our community. Beyond the contribution I hope to make, these youth inspire and renew my spirits. For one, they have so many fresh questions and dreams that are emerging at this time of their lives. For another, it is part of their teening process to explore and experiment.

Being a community health nurse, I have participated in many projects that have focused on teen development. Until recent years, I drew primarily on one model for community youth work: working on the problem-side. This model consists of first conducting a needs assessment, scoping out projects to meet the identified needs of the youth, and then measuring outcomes. While this approach has helped focus efforts and involve youth, I have always felt "bogged down" by the cumbersome infrastructure that this model carries. Even more, I have intuitively known that the youth experience the adult-identified projects as ones of "working on them," rather than evoking their potential and helping them develop their community leadership.

Until a small group of thoughtful community members took the time to reflect upon our socio-eco philosophy, I knew no other way. We went beyond looking at problems and reflected on the energy field behind the physical terrain of the land. We also looked at the elements that make up our town's history. It became obvious that our history was shaped through the wisdom of those who knew how to respond in harmony with the Greater Design of the land.

In our area of Kennett Square, we have learned through reflection that our land's energy field comes from following the way of *peaceful, progressive, inclusivity...* and this has become our living philosophy. New freedom and potential became unleashed when we finally understood that all community efforts have the highest potential when they take place under the umbrella of a living philosophy; we indeed have a higher order guidance for organizing ourselves.

Having a living philosophy as a starting point has become absolutely essential to our overall community work, including our work with the youth. The freedom I experience is one of knowing that we, each and all, are stewards of our community's living philosophy. This means no one "works on the youth" or "keeps them straight," but we all share in the responsibility of community work with the youth.

More and more, experience is showing me that the youth understand better than I do what is needed to help evolve our community. In our particular community we have many Mexican immigrants, and it is the bi-lingual children who take the lead in the family due to their parent's language barrier. These youth, along with the rest of the teens, have many ideas about how we could move forward as a community. The role of the adult has become one of challenging the teens to think of efforts and projects that will focus on potential and live our town's philosophy - this way they become partners in the co-creation of our town.

A recent example of this creation is when a group of high-school students took the lead to have a celebration with the students they tutored. Their aim was to design an event that honored the Study Buddy relationship that had developed throughout the year, validate a balance of work and play, and create a community building event. Being led by our town's philosophy, the students looked beyond the celebration to the sustaining community value of their work.

The students found a way to involve the church community where other tutoring efforts took place. They explored ways to validate some of the cultural celebration traditions of the students. Best of all, they reached out to other community groups and asked them to take on roles around their celebration's aim. They had high energy around the planning, and organized it mostly on their own. The measures of success were being placed on how they could take the spirit of *peaceful, progressive inclusivity* to the next edge, and not on how they could polish the event.

Later, I reflected on the satisfaction that we experienced from being a part of this community process together. The physical support for the event was provided, but the external details never got in the way of the guiding force - the energy field within which we were working. With this spiritual way of working together, our youth and community will continually grow to understand the importance of having the light of a living philosophy to lead the way.

The Potential of a Town's Living Philosophy

Never doubt that a small group of community-minded members can impact the turn of events in a town when they are leading from a living philosophy that is in concert with the socio-eco system. In our town of Kennett Square, PA, we have learned, through reflection, that we are in harmony with the energy of the land when we live by *peaceful, progressive, inclusivity.*

This philosophy was recently put to the test when a disenfranchised group brought a neighborhood issue to our town's governing body. They presented a list of concerns around behaviors of the Mexican residents living in a low-income apartment complex near their homes. Loud music, over-crowding and too many cars were disturbing the peace and quiet of the neighborhood. Let it be told that what started out as a "hot" enforcement issue moved into a community-building process.

The governing body took its cue from our town's living philosophy and quickly suggested that the concerns be more fully addressed at the following week's meeting, when the community space would be provided for many voices to be heard.

During the following week, thoughtful community members voluntarily took on the leadership role of asking, "How do we make this a meaningful process in order to peacefully progress as a community?" With this discernment, the leaders were able to identify all the key players. When invitations were given, there also was an expressed intent of bringing the next week's dialogue to a "higher level." This meant that the position would not be one of argument, but one of reflecting on the whole of our community towards better living out our philosophy.

On the following Monday evening, one by one, the landlord, enforcement officers, interpreters, advocates, and representatives from the home owners and apartment complex came to the front of the large community hall to express his or her view about the situation. The entire communication was delivered in Spanish and English. To some, this may have been cumbersome; to most, it was an opportunity to sit quietly and peacefully reflect on what was being said. The speaker also was required to wait for the translation, and then deliver focused thoughts to be once again interpreted - an unexpected gift in creating understanding.

With the groundwork laid for acting in a peaceful manner, the ideas for progressing beyond our current state started to unfold: "Let's have a neighborhood process where we learn about each other's culture and practices, or let's have a block party. Even better, let's develop a neighborhood core group which helps educate about ordinances and culture." These were just some of the ideas that started to bring new spirit and potential to the situation. The law enforcement issue was brought up, and yet it seemed that most realized that this would be an endless effort if the group did not work together as a whole and become more inclusive.

At present, we are moving forward. Some may wonder how this remarkable change came about. Others may just be relieved that it did not have a volatile outcome. For the core group of community members who helped bring about the meaningful process, they are grateful that they have learned the potential of coming from our town's living philosophy!

*Each is not
separate from,
above or outside
the larger
whole of life.*

Valuable Lessons in the Restraint

Staying focused on potential helps a community go beyond a restraint to the discovery of valuable lessons. In fact, there is a newfound freedom when one is willing to go beyond the surface to experience the energy and value being expressed in the restraint... and then build from this base.

A common human reaction is to label the restraint as negative, and to resist the message with as much force as possible. This approach drains energy and usually ends up creating more negativity - the very thing that one wants to eliminate. It takes a change of mind and intent to stop and reflect on the potential in all situations.

Recently, our local paper had an editorial that expressed the view that a community festival event had "outlived its initial vision." At first, this was experienced as a negative force that lacked appreciation. On further reflection, many lessons were revealed through this restraint by focusing on the potential behind the message.

As it was, out of respect for a long-time annual community event, a group of caring community members had picked up the baton from a previous committee. The planning process did not start from the energy or value of the event from the past, but focused on the functional roles within the committee. As a result, the festival ran well functionally, but missed the potential for having the event become a source of revitalization through a community-shared vision.

The heart of a festival is to bring new spirit to a town and to its people. It does this through tapping the essential energies of the whole community so that the celebration reflects the richness of the community. This small committee became alive when it reached this level of reflection on the essence of a festival; now they see the real potential of their role in the festival-making process... all sparked by the nudge of a restraint!

*Our heart is intended
and designed for
love to flow into
and through.*

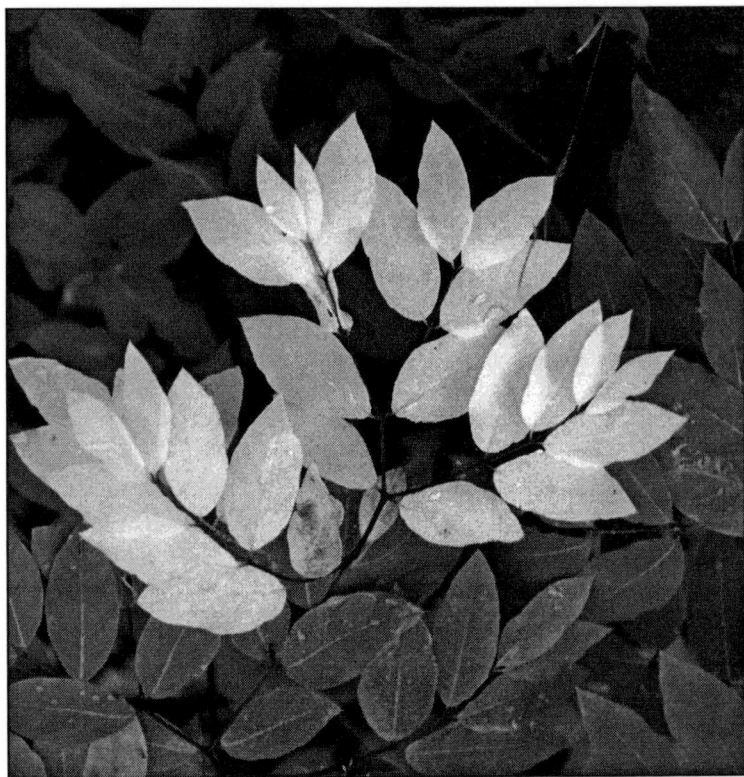

Path of Potential • P.O. Box 4058, Grand Junction, CO 81502 USA

Right for Each and All

Whenever a community conflict arises, it is easy to get pulled into the dynamics of the situation. Very quickly, a "pro" and "con" side is presented, and concerned community members rally around one side or the other. In reality, the problem has many tentacles that connect it to a larger picture, but this rarely gets explored.

It also is most disheartening when the conflict moves into a legal battle. In this event, individual or group rights become the focus, and the larger community conscience, dialogue and action are excluded from the picture. What then, is a community to do when the inevitable conflicts and positioning occur?

In the past few years, a small group of committed citizens have initiated a "reflection" process. They start from the whole of the community, and work from a level of repotentializing the heart of the community. This counter-culture does not ignore the problems of the town, but focuses on the value and potential of each of the parts of the whole community. The "rights" discussion becomes less individual; and in contrast, the subject is "what is most right" for each and all.

A case in point: As in any town, we have had several court cases where landlord and tenant rights are the subject of conflict. One can find advocates for each of these groups, and usually one or the other is found "at fault." When the community question became, "What is most right for each and all in this situation?" the picture became larger, and other elements of community life were activated.

Churches who had taken on the mission of mentoring youth in community volunteerism see potential in mentoring the youth in home repair. A public health nurse who has been mentoring families in parenting and life processes sees potential in providing a community learning experience. The landlord, who reports that he is constantly repairing the same broken door and window, sees potential in receiving help towards a sustained improved investment. The home supply store manager who cares about a viable business sees potential in donating outdated items. The tenant who reports that he or she does not have a responsive landlord for needed repairs sees potential in demonstrating a new pride and investment in a place called "home."

This group of individuals is working together as a whole system. In fact, its spirit and vitality is becoming a natural magnet for drawing in other elements of the community. Best of all, each is learning, in the midst of the challenge of "letting go" of one's own position, about the solving power of rising above community conflicts towards what is most right for each and all.

When we touch one member,
we touch all.

Winter 2004

Communicating
Images of Potential

As a mother of teenagers, I still recall sending off my newly licensed drivers with the message, "Now, don't get in a car accident!" Intuitively, this advice never felt right to me. Most of the time, I was left with images of ambulances, emergency rooms, and funeral homes.

It struck me one day that these words created the message of a problem, instead of what I was looking for - my child's safety. From that point on, my message on their departure became, "Stay safe!" It was amazing how this different phrase had the power of evoking in me a state of calm. I now was imaging them "wrapped in a bubble of safety" and we were starting from a position of potential, not problem.

As a health educator in my public health nursing role, I find that communicating the overall message of potential is key to helping clients develop healthier life patterns... not to mention the positive spirit this approach evokes in myself and in the clients and families.

Case in point: A pregnant woman is a cigarette smoker. In all health circles, she is viewed as having a serious health behavioral problem, and it is usually addressed with, "Let's talk about your cigarette smoking problem." Starting from this position evokes images of the nurse trying to fix someone, and trying to control another's behavior. On the other hand, if I start from the message of, "Let's talk about the things that will contribute to a healthy baby," it is easier to draw up images of fresh air and vigor and the promise of a nurse and client partnering process. Yes, we will eventually get to the smoking behavior, but it will be in the context of what we both share as a common goal - a healthy newborn!

Another example of starting from the image of potential comes when I am teaching parents how to handle a cantankerous toddler. Remembering to provide a message that gives the child a choice, i.e. "You may have this, this, or this," evokes the image of freedom within bounds. How much more promising for the parent and the child, instead of, "No, you may not have that!" Can you not just see the image a child must have in his head when the "no" word is shouted - a big mean giant putting its foot down for starters.

Recently, I made a home visit in response to a prenatal referral. The mother welcomed me graciously at the door and with a warm smile. I learned she had a dying child in the home with no hope of a cure. The child was carefully placed in the center of the bed and had several machines and tubes attached to her. I was lost for words because this seemed like an overwhelming tragedy! As I looked up at the mother, she took on the role of creating the image of potential that I hope to carry forward as she said, "This child is our angel sent from heaven, and every day she gives us love." I cannot think of a better image to hold!

Through reflection we receive an image of the good, right and effective working of the whole.

Path of Potential • P.O. Box 4058, Grand Junction, CO 81502 USA

Our Dialogue Group

Several years ago, we began a grassroots dialogue group in our community of Kennett Square, and named it "Each and All." Our Each and All Dialogue Group is very disciplined about meeting the first Wednesday of every month from 7:30 to 9 AM. We start on time, beginning with group quiet time to reflect on the energy of the land *(peaceful, progressive inclusivity)* and on the community that we all care about. Then we read articles from the "Path of Potential" Reader. This helps each of us to lift our thoughts to a higher level and to have a voice beyond ours to honor.

I have volunteered to plan and organize our gatherings. As the organizer, I pick out the articles with a theme that I believe relates to the current state of our community that month. For example, our session in January was related to peace and harmony because we were organizing a huge event for Martin Luther King Day. I pull from articles across all the Readers. After reading/hearing an article, each person (who wishes to) shares with the group how they believe it pertains to our community... and how we can extend it. We ask the questions: What is the seed we need to plant? Who do we connect with to help plant that seed? How will this extend the living philosophy of our land: *peaceful, progressive, inclusivity?*

The more we reflect,
the greater the potential for accessing wisdom.

Path of Potential • P.O. Box 4058, Grand Junction, CO 81502 USA

Spring 2004

A Town's Living Philosophy - Bridge to Community Potential

In our town, the story continues to be told that our "Bridging the Community" meetings are the secret to building a dynamic community. This spirited and inspired grassroots process is now in its eighth year in Kennett Square, Pa.

Each and all are welcome to attend these bi-monthly meetings held at a different community site each time. Walking into the door of the community gathering, it soon becomes clear that each person is appreciated for their unique role that is played; status, money, age, creed and race are not the determining factors in being valued.

How is this community state of being evoked? In our "bridging" meetings, we start from our town's living philosophy, which is reflective of the energy and make-up of the land where we reside. In our community of Kennett, the land tells us that we are called to live from the philosophy of *peaceful, progressive, inclusivity.*

Starting from this ground, we move forward in the meeting, exploring creative ways to "bridge" community needs with resources. In all our efforts, we take direction from our living philosophy. The spirit of harmonizing with our land's virtue becomes a uniting force; barriers are broken down, and new potential is released. Wouldn't it be great if every town discovered this natural process for community building?

*Roles and work are the means by which
we unfold potential and make it real.*

 Path of Potential • P.O. Box 4058, Grand Junction, CO 81502 USA

Uncovering the
Work of the Heart

As a Community Health Nurse, I am presented with issues concerning basic needs on a daily basis. It always has been my nature to take on the responsibility myself and ask, "What can I do about this?" In uncovering the work of the heart, my question has evolved to, "What is the best role for me to play, and who else needs to be involved?" Allowing this space for reflection has opened up a whole new way of nursing care.

In a broader sense, I am learning that the most meaningful heartfelt response to basic needs is addressing them within a community process that is larger than the individual - a response that opens the door to each and all to be part of the solution. Are we not all a part of something larger than ourselves?

One of the approaches we have initiated in our town is the Bridging the Community process. This open door meeting invites all community residents to attend. We enter as "we... the community," instead of "them" and "us," and learn about community needs as well as our many resources.

It is here where the request for beds for new migrant farm-workers is brought up; it is here where tutoring help and snacks for after-school programs is offered; it is here where the recipients of these benefits discover arenas where they can offer their unique talents and take on a contributing role. It is an equal playing field where every person becomes a giver and a receiver.

Today, when I receive a call to help out with a basic need, I invite the person or group to a "bridging" meeting, or refer them to a person that I met at a "bridging" meeting. When I am trying to understand all the players in the food, housing and clothing arenas, I attend a "bridging" meeting. When I am trying to empower a person to find his or her work of the heart, I invite them to a "bridging" meeting.

My nursing role has moved beyond taking on the responsibility myself to being a steward of a community process, where sharing the work uncovers one LOVING COMMUNITY HEART!

Taking the Lead from Our History

Kennett Square is a *peaceful, progressive and inclusive* community - our history tells us so!

Linden Street is a wonderful example of coming to terms with our town's history and allowing it to be its guide. Last year, residents uncovered a home on their street that once sheltered underground slaves. They learned that this "inclusive" act of long ago led to the first black homeowner in Kennett Square. Linden Street residents are now taking leadership and moving forward with a plan to bring back the power of the street.

Another example of living in harmony with our town's spirit occurred when the mushroom growers felt the hard reality of price pressures from abroad. Instead of being beaten, they created a higher value product - fresh exotic mushrooms. Thanks to their leadership, Kennett still has a strong economic base.

For the past year, caring community members have been inspired by the town's history, and have taken the lead to address the education of new Mexican residents and homeowners in the Stenning Hills area. Mexican bi-lingual youth have created educational flyers and conducted one-on-one interactions with the new residents. Residents have opened up their homes to neighborhood meetings to explore creative ways to be "good neighbors." The Martin Luther King Community Breakfast Committee has awarded monies to grassroots efforts to nourish peaceful solutions in Stenning Hills. La Comunidad Hispana offers bilingual staff to translate, interpret and educate the new residents in town. All of these efforts have the potential to transform Stenning Hills.

We are a town with a proud history. We are a town that has made its major changes through the people... and not through tighter governance. We are a town whose hearts and minds are inspired by our history of being *peaceful, progressive and inclusive.*

 Path of Potential • P.O. Box 4058, Grand Junction, CO 81502 USA

Through opening the heart,
we see and experience
the essence of each and all.

Reflections from Each and All Dialogue Group

The Each and All Dialogue Group is a diverse group of community members who meet monthly to reflect on the path of potential in the context of the living philosophy of Kennett Square, PA. The dialogue recently focused on the need for stopping one's automatic behaviors and learning to manage one's actions towards choices that manifest the land's virtue: our living philosophy of *peaceful progressive inclusivity.*

There is a lesson to be learned from each person's reflection:

A Rotarian sees the importance of moving from "quick fix" solutions to thinking from a "four generations" perspective. He knows that his choices will carry out the living philosophy if he considers the impact of his actions through time... those affecting his children, his children's children, and onward.

A Film Maker reflects on how easy it is to "get caught up in one's own scene." His favorite means for focusing the lens is to say to himself, "And... this is not about you."

A Musician tells a story about being a teacher and ending up becoming a student. His means of self-managing is to work on the qualities of patience and detachment, which in turn help him become a finely tuned instrument for living the philosophy of the land.

An Investment Banker speaks about how his job goes

beyond getting new accounts. With this awareness, he joins the spirit of each customer and makes plans which include the many elements that make up the whole of a person's life.

A Non-Profit Fundraiser reflects on how he is moving beyond collecting money as his goal to one of investing community members' hearts and minds in the larger community.

A Mother speaks about parenting a teen with this living philosophy, and moving from disciplining as the focus to helping evoke in her son his greater potential and expanded horizons.

A Nurse sees the importance of moving beyond her solo caretaker role to one of creating a process that "bridges the elements of the community" ...which in turn builds a community circle of caring.

EACH person making a conscious choice to change old behaviors... ALL focusing on *peaceful, progressive, inclusivity.*

*Inherent within our design
is a yearning to pursue essential truths,
discover meaning, and fulfill our life's purpose.*

Path of Potential • P.O. Box 4058, Grand Junction, CO 81502 USA

A Living Philosophy -
Work of the Heart

The days are over when I would ask myself, "Am I really doing the work of my heart?" I have always had a strong desire to be instrumental in leaving the world a better place; the question was always, "How?" This serious question, which started from a very young age, is now being satisfied.

Looking back, I can see that until I took on a living philosophy, and then the leadership role of helping a community live from this frame of reference, I was lost. It is now evident to me that a living philosophy provides the container from which a person and a community make choices to express and develop themselves.

The living philosophy I am choosing to live by comes from the land where I live. Taking the time to reflect with others, I was able to appreciate the qualities of the living area that we share. Indeed, one can experience the innate energies of a particular place if one is intentional and willing to go beyond one's senses to the energy world.

The best part of this exercise is seeing how these energetic qualities resonate with our inner spirit and being. When we finally put the words of *peaceful, progressive,* inclusivity as the special virtue of our land, we had a living philosophy to lead the way. In essence, this helped us to see how each one of us could now whole-heartedly work to fulfill our role in the unfolding plan of the Creator.

Community is essential to uncovering the path of our calling...

and realizing our potential as we pursue that path.

Path of Potential • P.O. Box 4058, Grand Junction, CO 81502 USA

Building Our
Practical Living Philsophy

Path of Potential • P.O. Box 4058, Grand Junction, CO 81502 USA

Quality of life is a natural pursuit, and therefore seemingly intended. Ultimately, however, the essence of our design is to seek and live out a meaningful life... a path not always free from struggle and travail, but a path that gets clearer as we gain glimpses of our purpose and instrumentality.

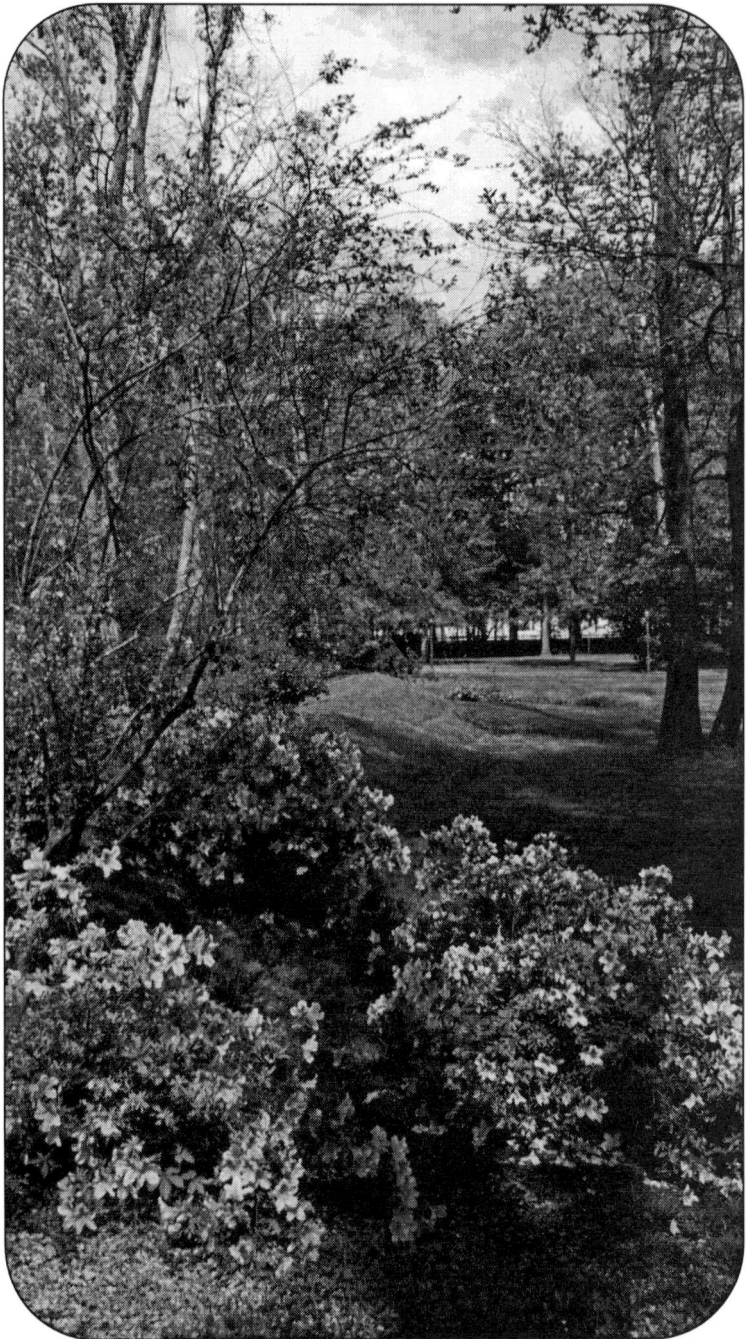

186   *Path of Potential* • P.O. Box 4058, Grand Junction, CO 81502 USA

Introduction

A Search for Meaning

We know from experience – and through reflecting on our experience – that each stage of life brings with it a particular nature of questions. We discover these questions are always present, if not in the foreground of our thought, then at the very least in the readily accessible background. We find they are the common subject matter for discussion and exploration with like-minded others.

One such stage occurs as we are entering into and living out young adulthood. Here it is quite common to live with questions such as "Who am I? Why am I here? What do I want to become? What do I need to become?" These questions are never totally satisfied; they show up ongoingly throughout our lives, and they call us to conscientiously work toward their answer.

Accompanying these questions is the real task of building for oneself a frame of reference – an orderly thought base from which to live... a frame of reference we can call upon and reflect against as we make our way into a world different from the one experienced by the "elders" who have been guiding us. This new thought base seeks not to discard essential truths, but rather to make them real – truly relevant – in the dynamic and emerging world we are being called upon to shape and create. We sense that in the absence of a real, practical, working frame of reference – a frame of reference that ongoingly aids in seeing essential truths – we will lose our opportunity to be and become... and instead be caught up in, defined by, and swept away by past sameness. Defining our world and ourselves by what is and what has been, we have no possibility of experiencing the joy of realizing our potential to become – to live out and manifest our essence as our uniqueness.

A frame of reference that is real and relevant to the dynamics and drama of the time in which we are living, and one that reflects our inherent urge or call to become, is a living philosophy. A living philosophy of life is one that we can live from and be disciplined about, that acknowledges the reality of our current situation, and that enables the realization of the open-ended potential of each and all... a philosophy that is personal, yet one that operates in service of the larger wholes within which we live – our communities, society, the whole of life. A living philosophy of life both comes from potential and has the potential to bring about a wholeness and unity of family, community and humanity previously unimaginable. As such, it is a people's philosophy because it flows through and among the people through reflection and dialogue, guided by purpose and principles, acted on and carried out by heartfelt roles and expressions.

What follows here is written to provide food for reflection and dialogue – the nature of reflection and dialogue that contributes to creating one's own personal living philosophy of life... a philosophy that encompasses one's own life, as well as the whole of life.

There is a Source
...an ongoing Source of creation.

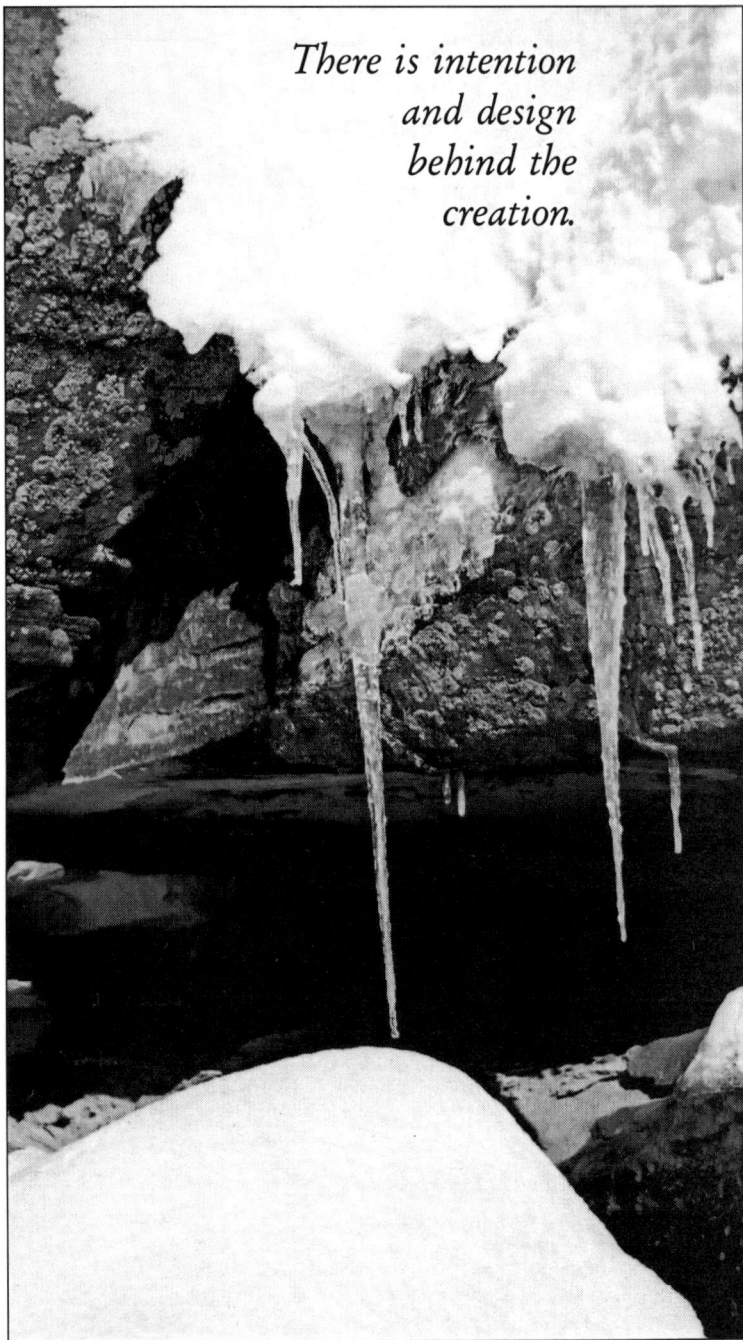

There is intention
and design
behind the
creation.

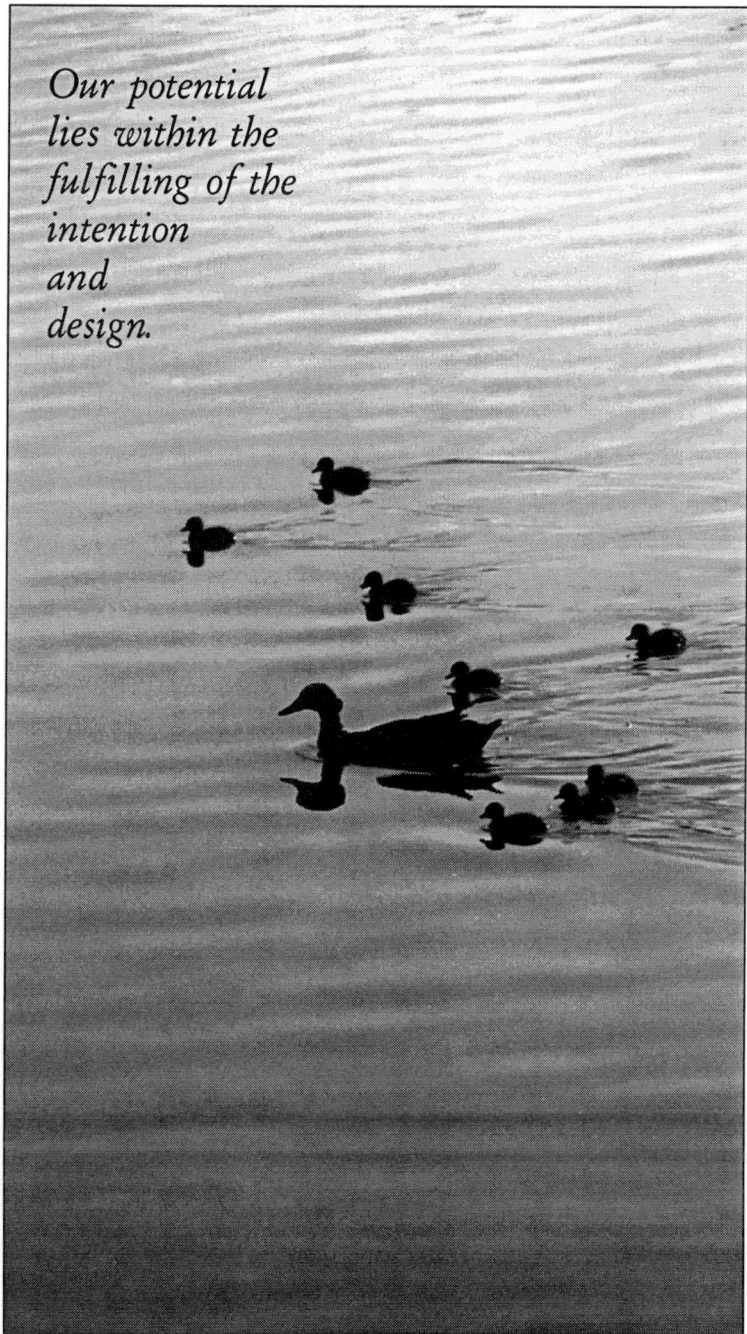

Our potential
lies within the
fulfilling of the
intention
and
design.

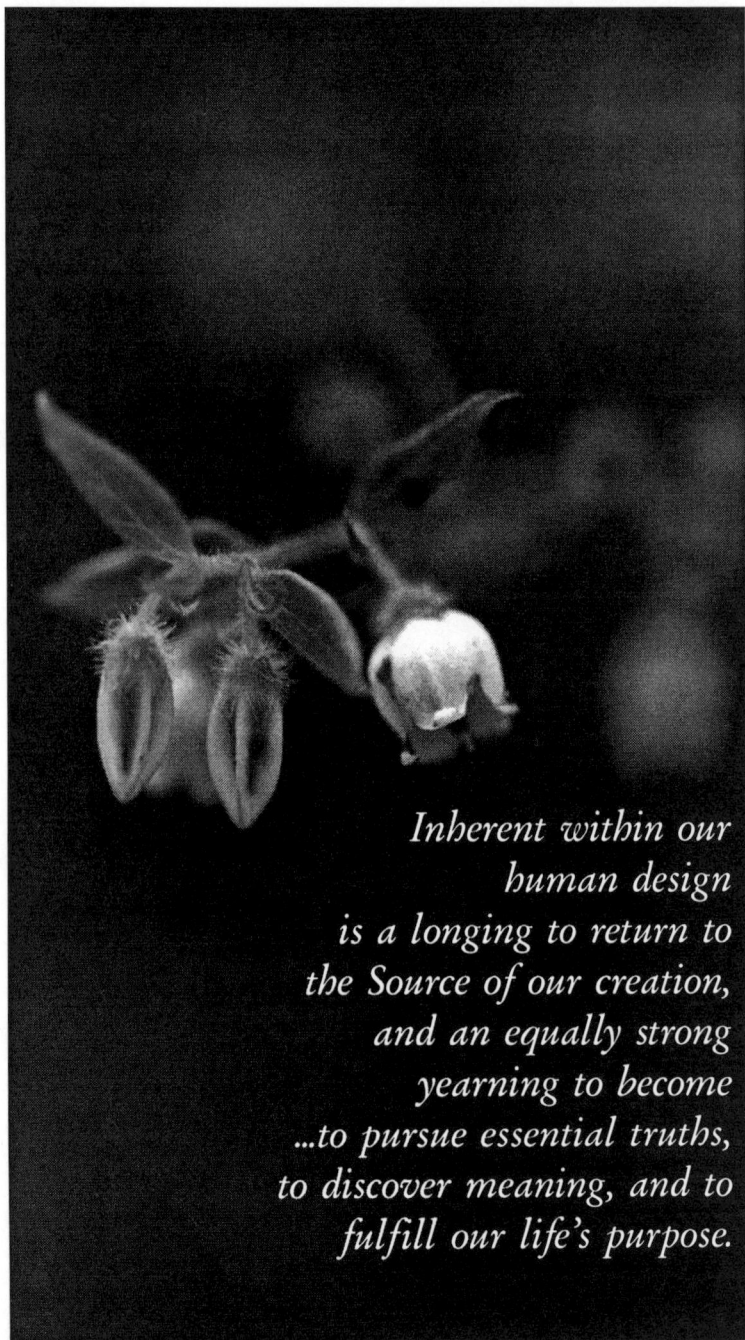

Inherent within our human design is a longing to return to the Source of our creation, and an equally strong yearning to become ...to pursue essential truths, to discover meaning, and to fulfill our life's purpose.

Path of Potential • P.O. Box 4058, Grand Junction, CO 81502 USA

A living philosophy of life - a disciplined way of living and working in harmony with life processes - illuminates the path of becoming ...a path in harmony with the intention of the Creator.

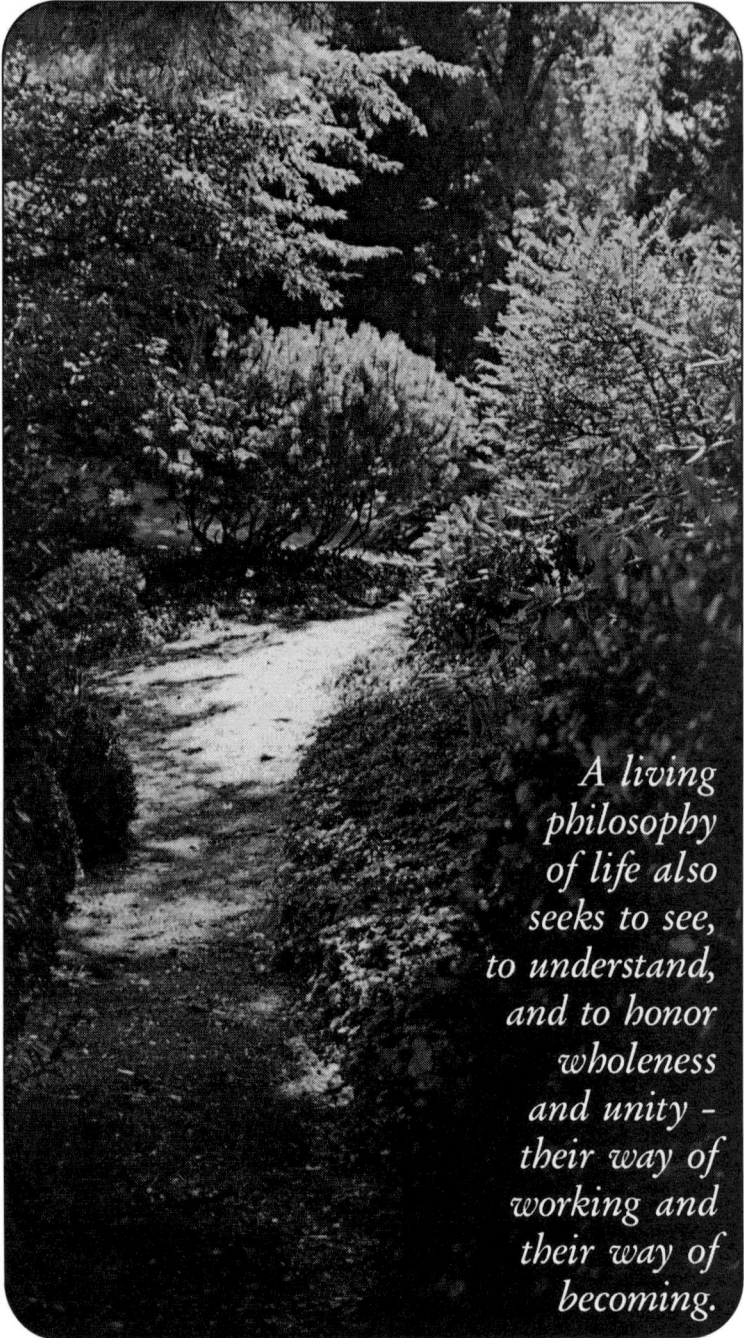

*A living
philosophy
of life also
seeks to see,
to understand,
and to honor
wholeness
and unity –
their way of
working and
their way of
becoming.*

194

Living Philosophy often finds itself to be a complementary partner with theologies that take on the work of illuminating the way of returning - the fulfilling of our longing to return to the Source of our creation.

*Living philosophy readily
resonates with sciences and
scientific approaches that seek
understanding and knowledge
of the design and purpose of
life's manifestations -
those living sciences anchored
in systemic working and
wholeness.*

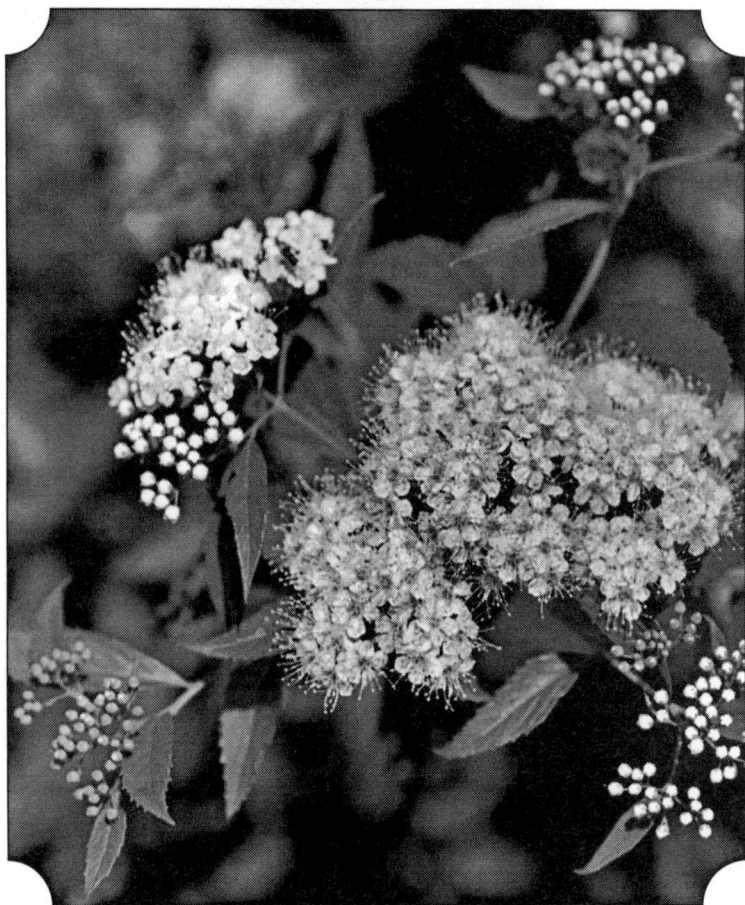

Path of Potential • P.O. Box 4058, Grand Junction, CO 81502 USA

We, the people of earth,
were created and are
intentionally designed
as living creatures -
creatures of life.

Life itself has purpose; and we, like other systemic members of life, also have purpose, and therefore a role in the working and ongoingness of life's processes on earth.

Path of Potential • P.O. Box 4058, Grand Junction, CO 81502 USA

*Fulfilling
our intended
role in the
working
and
ongoingness*
*of life, we manifest and
realize our potential
...and by so doing,
become fully and truly human.*

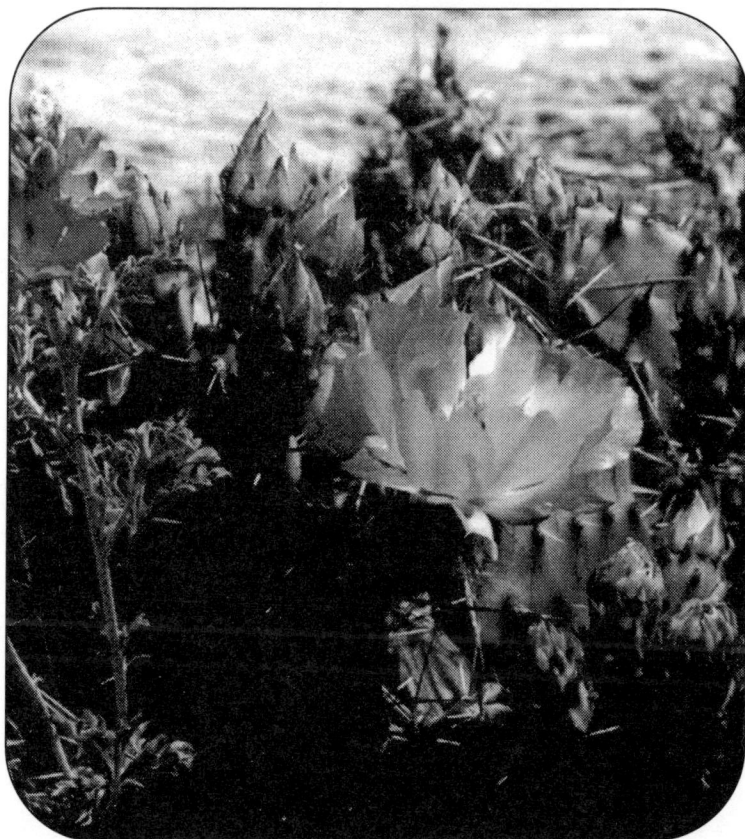

Life is created with open-ended potential; being members of life, we too are imbued with open-ended potential.

    Path of Potential • P.O. Box 4058, Grand Junction, CO 81502 USA

While life
is designed to
have a myriad
of possibilities,
true potential
lies along the
path of intention -
the intention
behind
the whole
of creation.

Reflection and dialogue are
the means of
"seeing"
true potential.

 Path of Potential • P.O. Box 4058, Grand Junction, CO 81502 USA

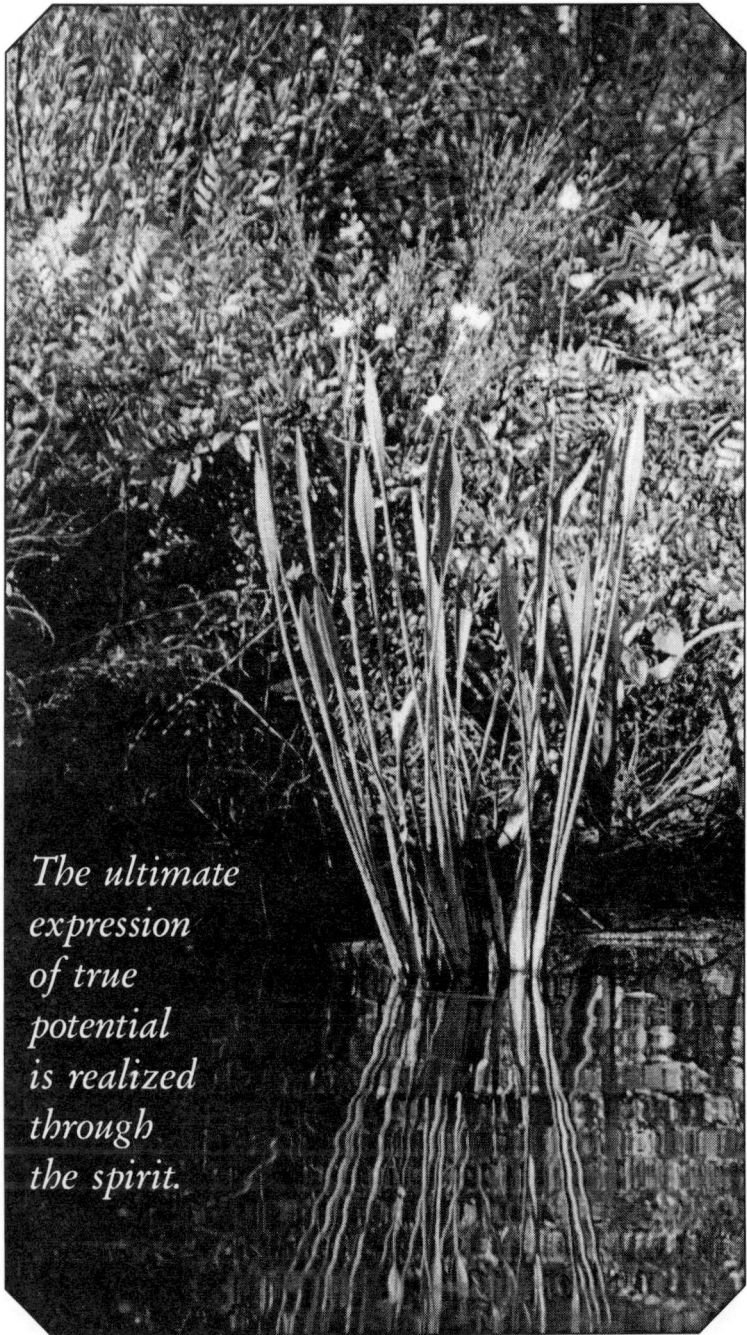

The ultimate
expression
of true
potential
is realized
through
the spirit.

Life is not the source of spirit,
but rather an instrument for the
manifestation
of spirit –
the will
force
of the
Creator.

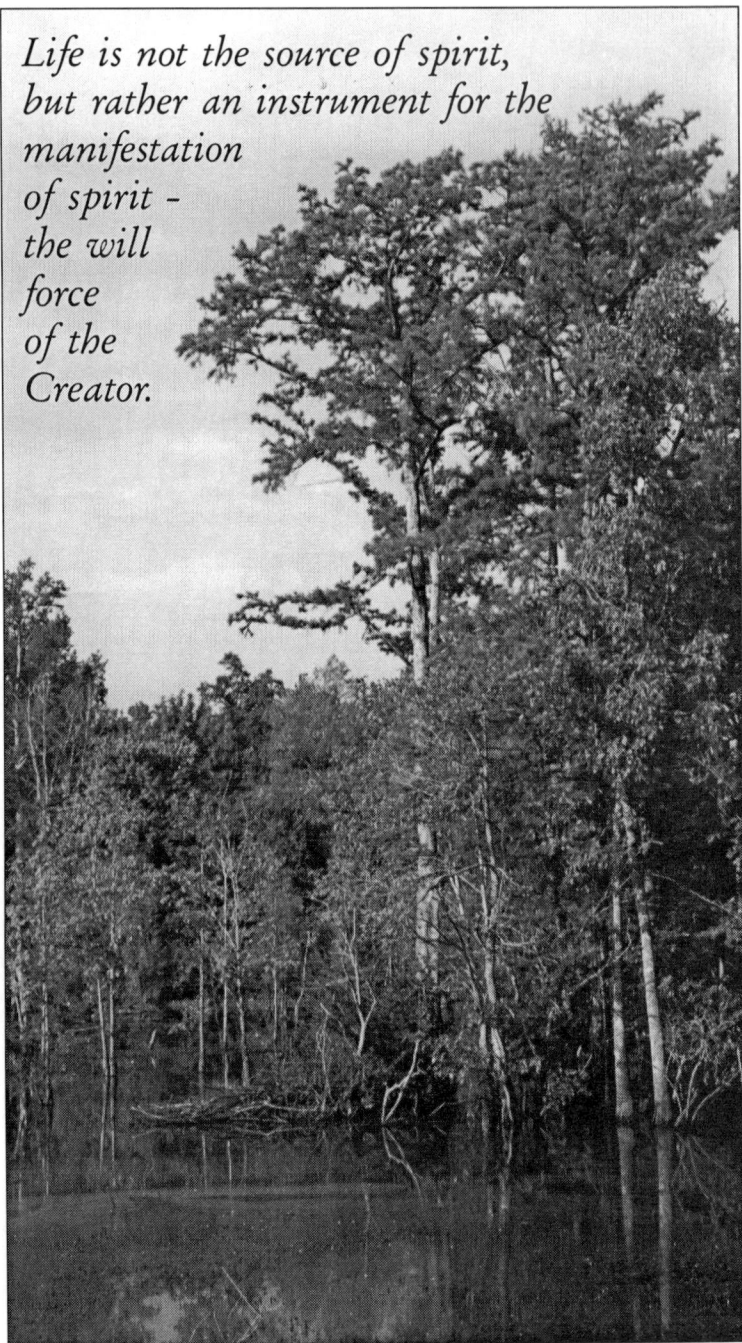

The spirit enters into,
through,
and is flavored by
essence patterns -
the inbuilt possibility
through which
life's intended work
is carried out.

Within
each and all
of life's members
lies an essence –
an essential pattern.

Path of Potential • P.O. Box 4058, Grand Junction, CO 81502 USA

*Essence patterns are the means through
which the will and spirit
of the Creator
enter into
the living and working
processes of life.*

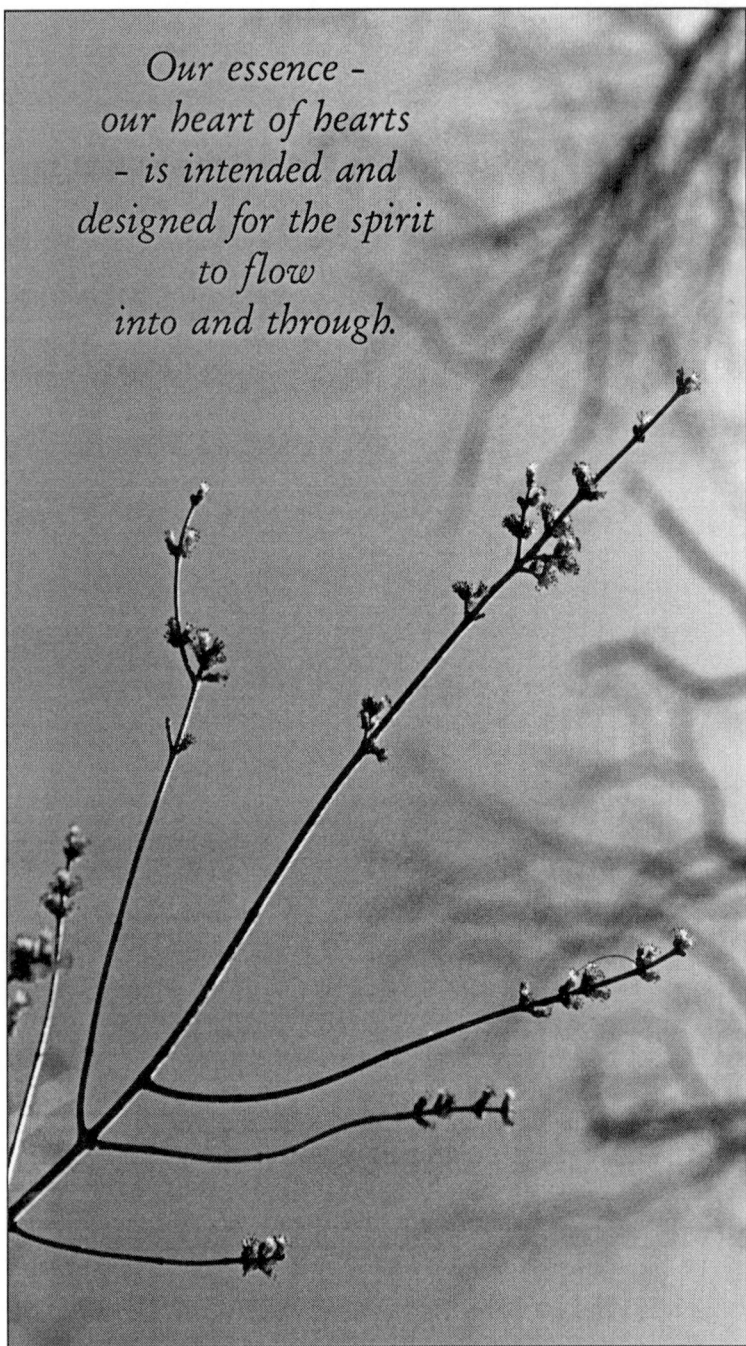

Our essence -
our heart of hearts
- is intended and
designed for the spirit
to flow
into and through.

Path of Potential • P.O. Box 4058, Grand Junction, CO 81502 USA

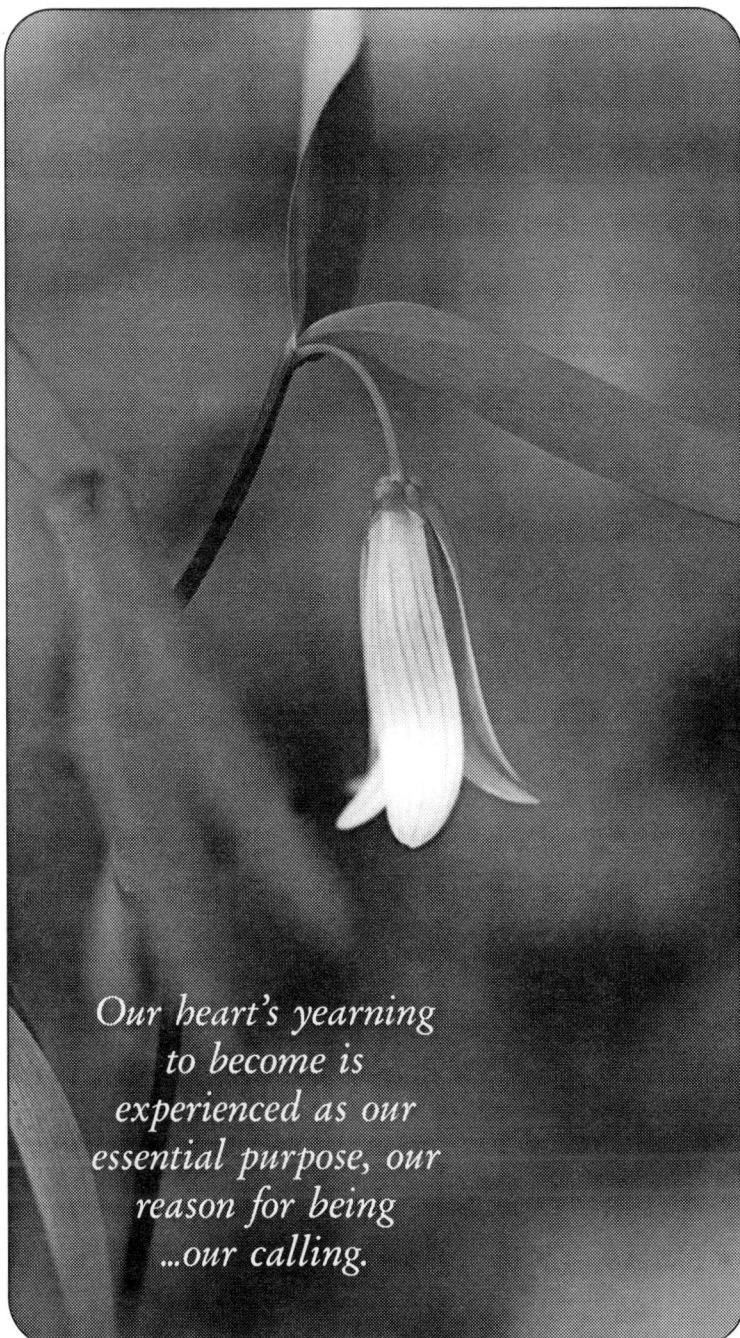

*Our heart's yearning
to become is
experienced as our
essential purpose, our
reason for being
...our calling.*

Our calling carries us
beyond the restraints
of who we think
or imagine we are...

...to the
freedom
of who we
can be
and what
we can
become.

210   *Path of Potential* • P.O. Box 4058, Grand Junction, CO 81502 USA

Community is essential to uncovering the path of our calling and realizing our potential as we pursue that path.

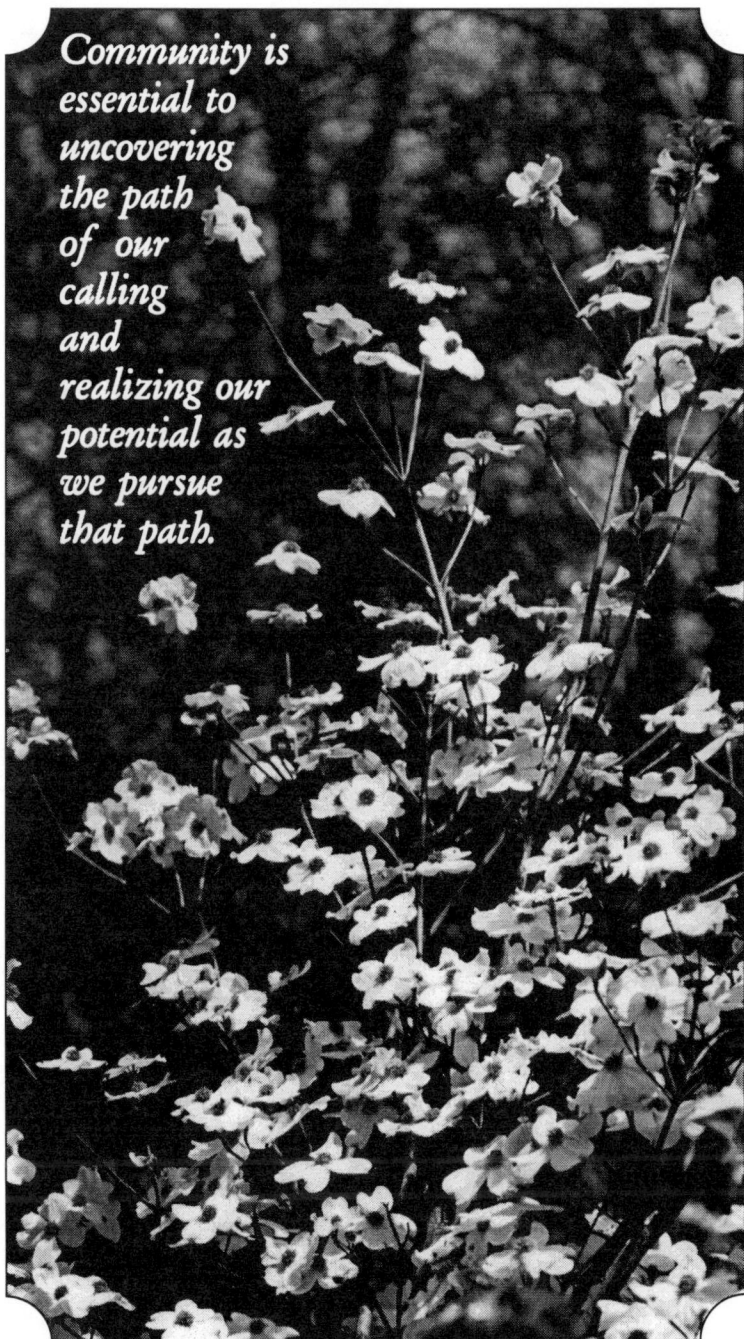

When we surrender to
our calling -
   take up our work and
   role within the family
      of life on earth -
spirit can be
manifested.

    Path of Potential • P.O. Box 4058, Grand Junction, CO 81502 USA

*When carried out,
our essential purpose
results in a spirit
manifested, thus
ensuring the
presence of the
will of the Creator
in the evolutionary
processes of
earth and life.*

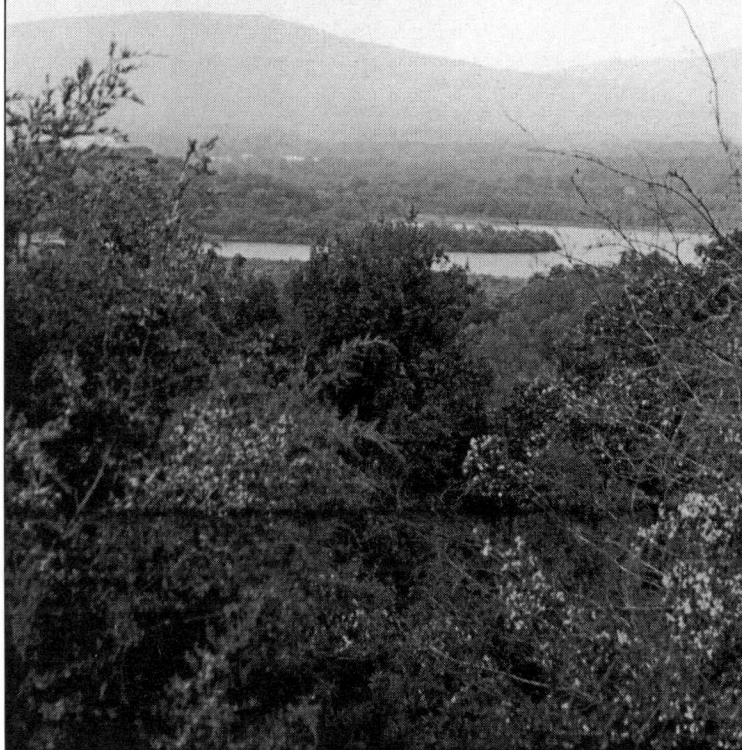

*Our role in the unfolding plan
of the Creator extends both
to and beyond the
human family to
include the
whole of life.*

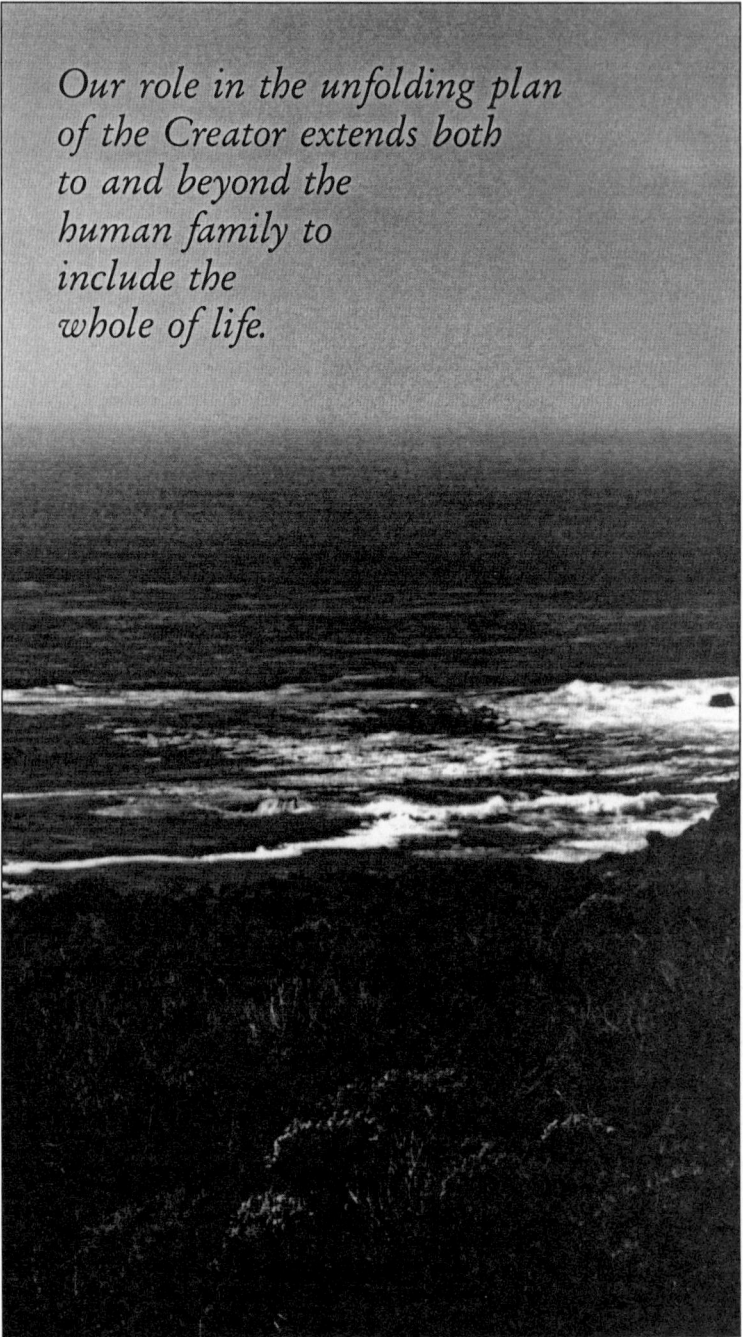

Path of Potential • P.O. Box 4058, Grand Junction, CO 81502 USA

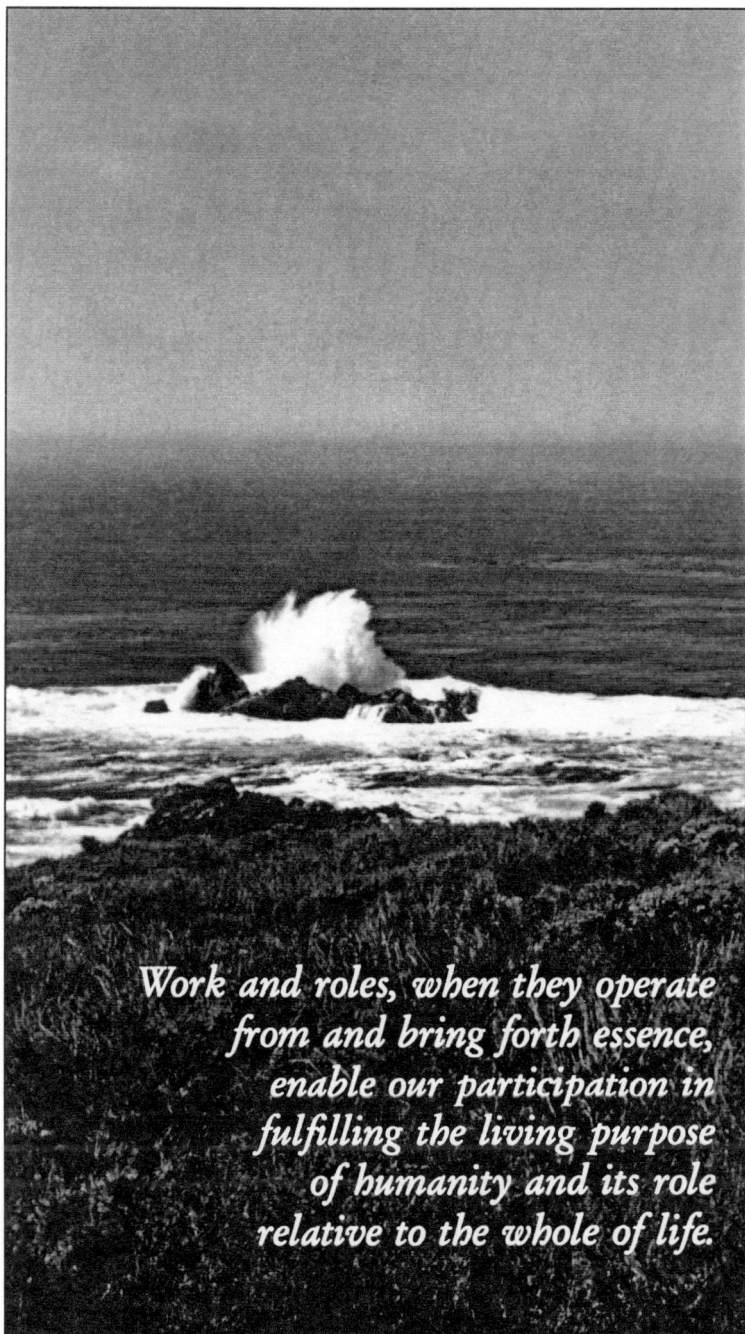

Work and roles, when they operate
from and bring forth essence,
enable our participation in
fulfilling the living purpose
of humanity and its role
relative to the whole of life.

Path of Potential • P.O. Box 4058, Grand Junction, CO 81502 USA

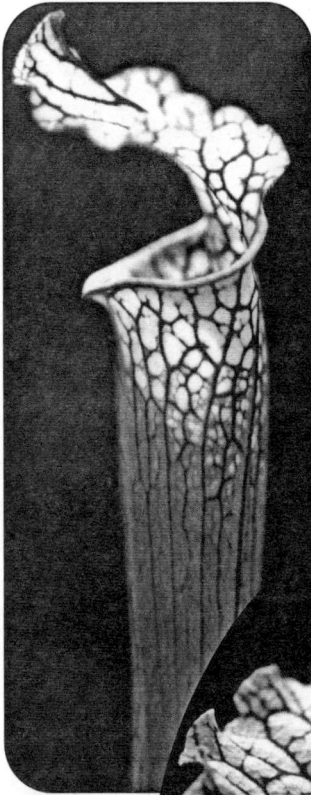

*A heart that becomes
an instrument for the
working of the spirit
of the Creator
- a spirit manifested -
is available to all of life
forever ...and herein lies
our truest potential.*

It is possible - within the scope of our design - to live and work in ways that are beyond sustaining ourselves and our lives ...to live and work in ways that enable unfolding and realizing the potential of life, life's community, and life's members.

Path of Potential • P.O. Box 4058, Grand Junction, CO 81502 USA

Critical to fulfilling our individual purpose and the purpose of the human family is the recognition and acceptance that we are not the source...

...we are intended and uniquely designed as instruments. As such, we have the inherent capacity to be subject to and cooperate with the unfolding plan of creation.

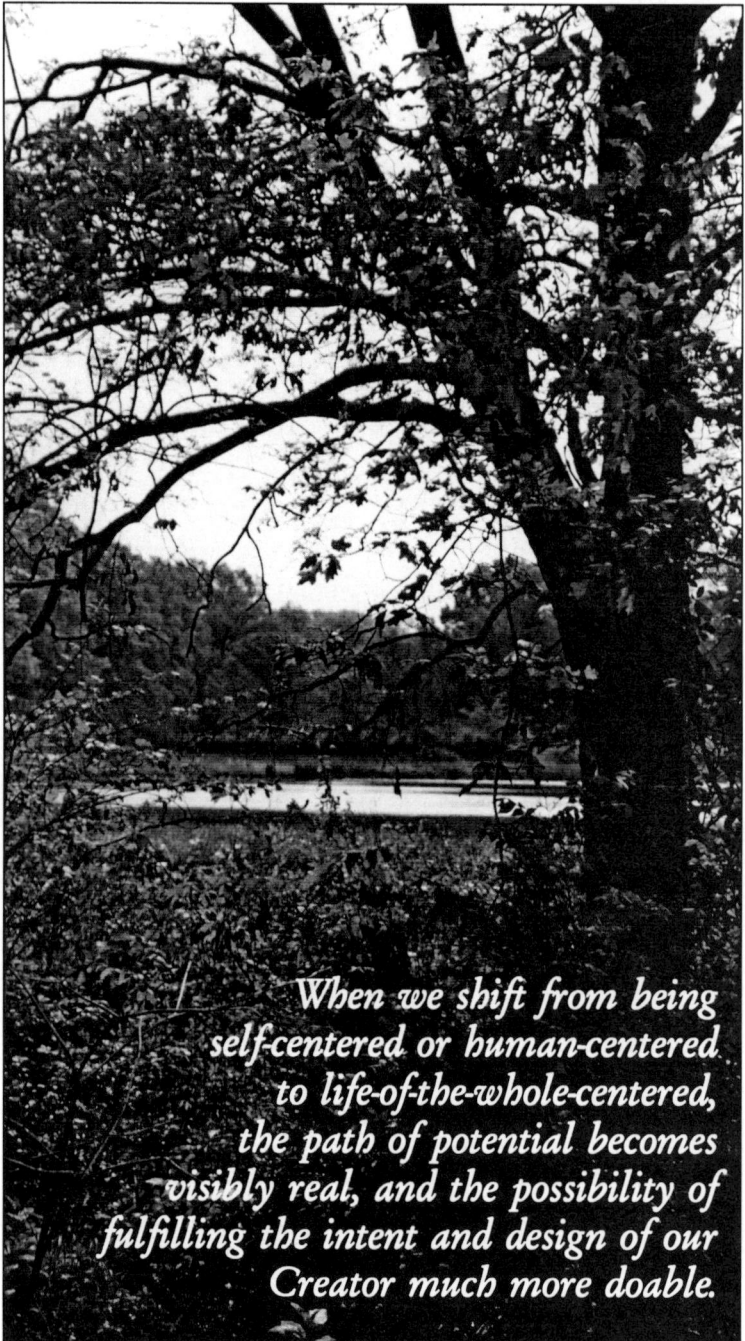

When we shift from being
self-centered or human-centered
to life-of-the-whole-centered,
the path of potential becomes
visibly real, and the possibility of
fulfilling the intent and design of our
Creator much more doable.

Path of Potential • P.O. Box 4058, Grand Junction, CO 81502 USA

*Life on earth is
ordered in,
organized by,
and progresses
within energy
fields; as
living beings,
we are
designed
and
intended
to
harmonize
and
resonate
with the
Creator's
earthly
energy
fields.*

We can, with right "tuning" on our part, experience the virtue of a particular energy field of earth; we can gain a true and real "sense of place."

This characteristic shows up in our references to people of the plains, the desert, the mountains, the tundra, and on and on.

Path of Potential • P.O. Box 4058, Grand Junction, CO 81502 USA

As we tune our
unique essence
into a particular
earthly energy
field, we become
working, acting,
contributing parts
of the ongoing
working of the whole of life.

A harmonious concert of spirit
emerges from the
simultaneous
manifesting
of essences...

...a concert
in which life's members
tune themselves with the essence of
their surrounding energy field.

Path of Potential • P.O. Box 4058, Grand Junction, CO 81502 USA

Humankind has a role as a true working partner in sustaining the nourishing power of earth, and in the realization of earth's purpose - serving as a place for life to flourish.

*Our essential role and work is a
particular manifestation of our
essence pattern of potentiality,
called forth through
the will of the Creator.*

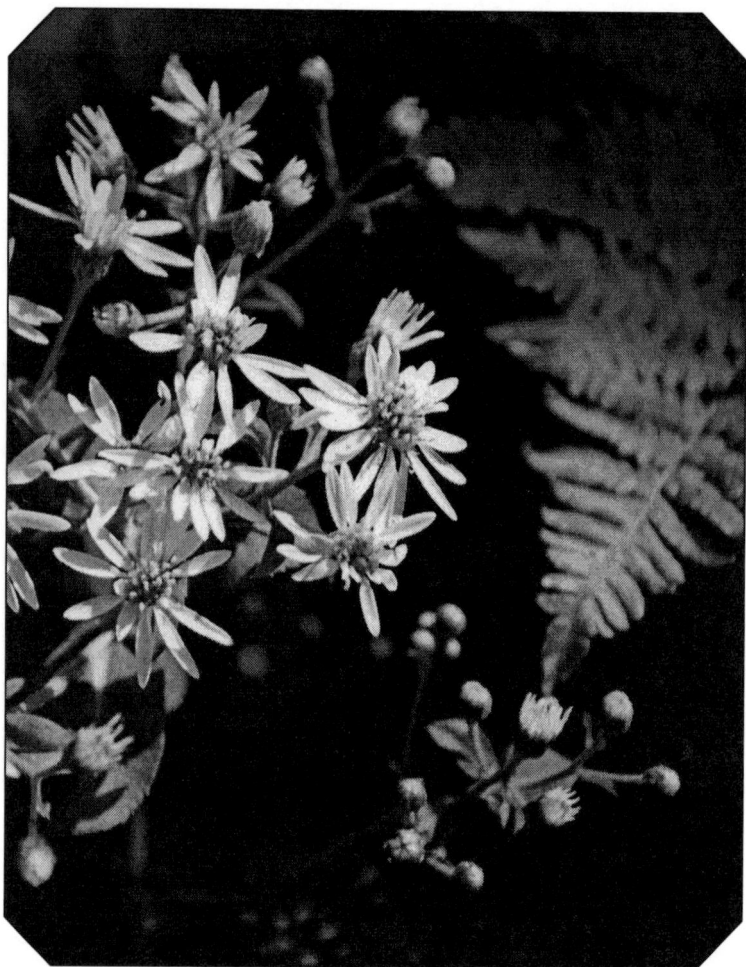

Path of Potential • P.O. Box 4058, Grand Junction, CO 81502 USA

*The process of becoming
is one of being true to one's heart
and staying connected to and
increasingly on the path of our calling.*

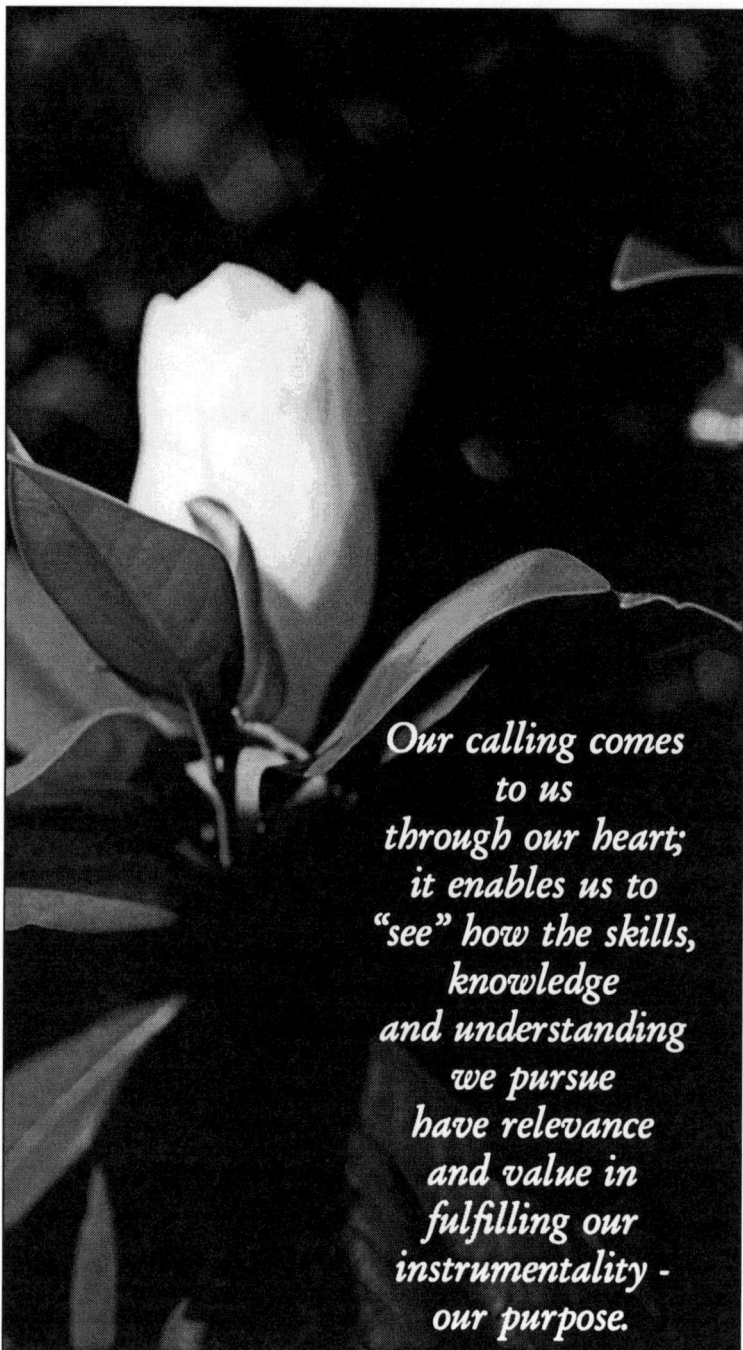

*Our calling comes
to us
through our heart;
it enables us to
"see" how the skills,
knowledge
and understanding
we pursue
have relevance
and value in
fulfilling our
instrumentality -
our purpose.*

Path of Potential • P.O. Box 4058, Grand Junction, CO 81502 USA

While becoming,
we strive to gain
discerning capacity
so that the choices we make -
that which we select from the
multitude of possibility -
are along the path of our potential,
and intrinsically in harmony
with our conscience.

While becoming,
we willfully choose
possibilities congruent
with essence and
potential,
and we resist
temptations of
possibilities that
appear and
actually may be more
advantageous
in regards
to our existence.

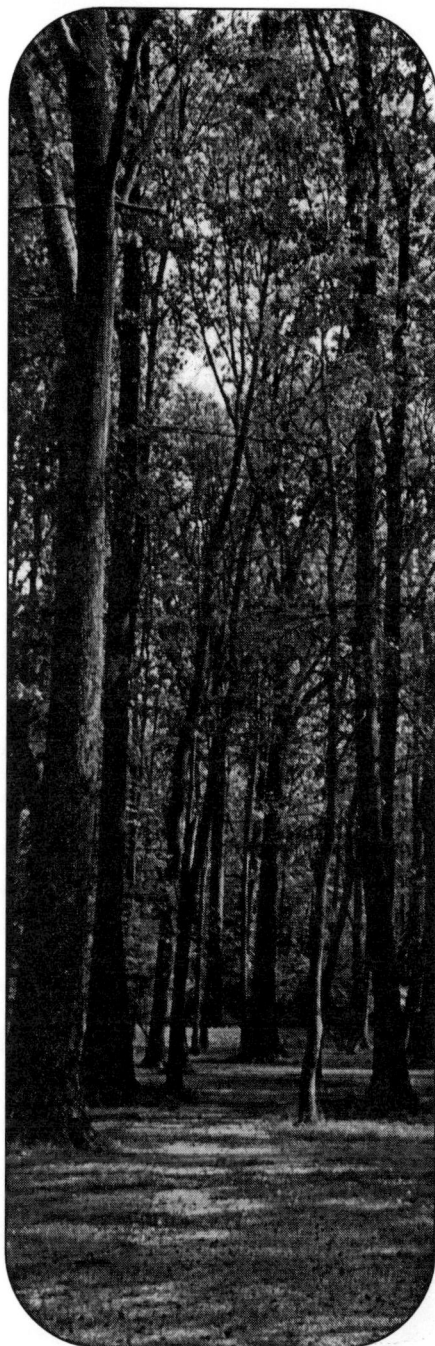

When we shift our efforts and attention away from hierarchical position and personal advantage toward roles that require discovery and manifestation of essence and uniqueness, life for us becomes very real ...and work becomes a source of meaning and dignity in our lives.

In essence and in
spirit,
no one
person
is above another
...we are
in truth
all equal.

Path of Potential • P.O. Box 4058, Grand Junction, CO 81502 USA

*Each essence is unique. These
differentiations reflect the truth of our
equality and are manifested
(not in hierarchies, but)
through roles -
roles that acknowledge the realness of the
work to be done, and the significance of
each part played.*

Rather than shy away from or build artificial protective boundaries against the processes of life, our work as humankind is to fully embrace, deeply taste, and wholeheartedly experience - through its stages, phases, agonies and ecstasies - the whole of life.

Path of Potential • P.O. Box 4058, Grand Junction, CO 81502 USA

*Embracing and fully
experiencing the
agonies and
ecstasies of life,
we come to know
meaning and share
in the awe and wonder
of that which
makes life real.*

The source of significance is spirit. The spirit enters and flows through us as we engage in the work of discovering our purpose, taking on essential roles, and answering our calling; it is through the pursuit and acceptance of this work that spirit is manifested.

Path of Potential • P.O. Box 4058, Grand Junction, CO 81502 USA

The process of deepening the understanding of our role and increasing our level of cooperation occurs through the receptivity produced by reflection and dialogue.

Reflection
and dialogue produce
a deeper, clearer and more complete
sense of the rightness and goodness of
actions along the path on which our
hearts seem to be guiding us.

Path of Potential • P.O. Box 4058, Grand Junction, CO 81502 USA

*Reflection
and dialogue are the means
by which we can prepare ourselves
to hear when our hearts
are being spoken to
...to hear the voice of wisdom.*

Through reflection and dialogue, the community gains access to ways of being and doing that were previously unimaginable... or believed to be impossible.

Path of Potential • P.O. Box 4058, Grand Junction, CO 81502 USA

Through reflection and dialogue,
we are given images of ways of being
and doing in harmony with
the Creator's intent for life -
our life, life of the community,
and life of the whole.

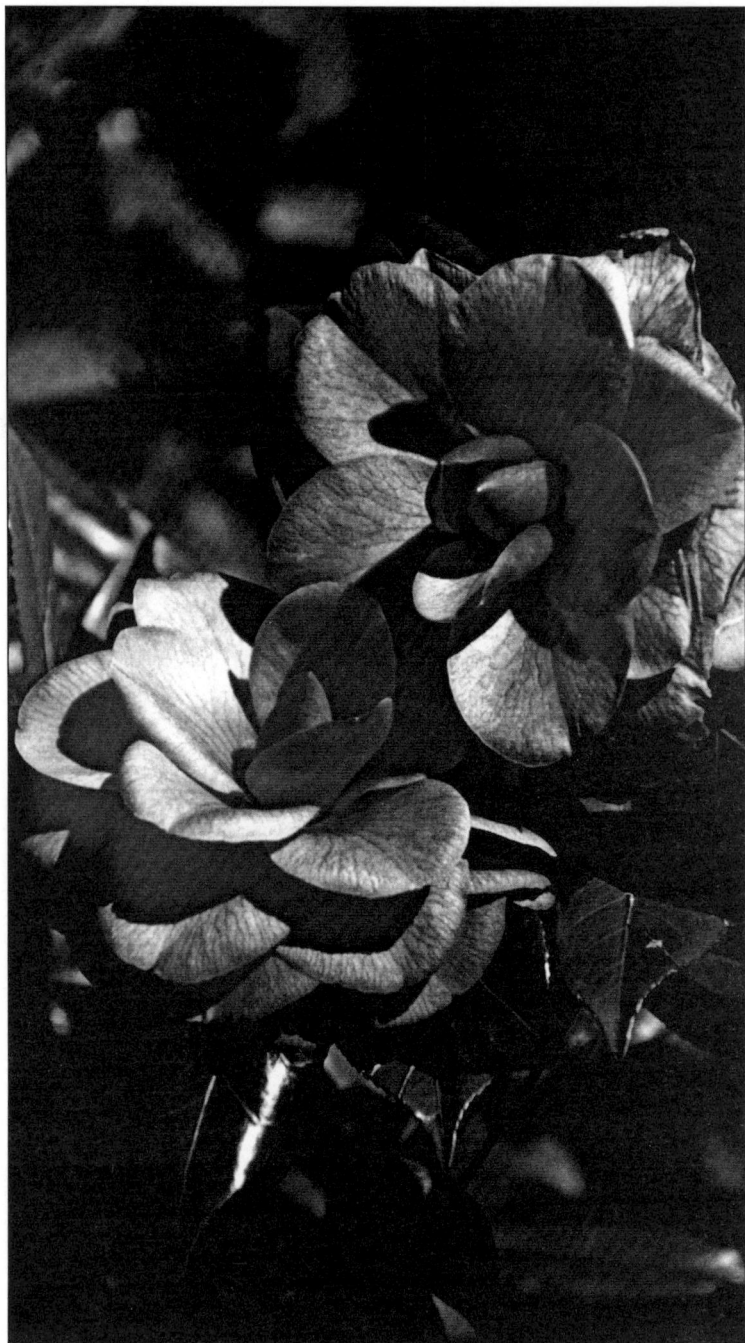

Path of Potential • P.O. Box 4058, Grand Junction, CO 81502 USA

Getting Dialogue Started

Should your reflection stir the notion of wanting to join with others in dialogue for the purpose of building personal life philosophies, here are some thoughts on getting started.

There are as many ways of creating a practical living philosophy as there are people. Yet all require reflection and dialogue – reflective interaction with others who are also pursuing for themselves a philosophy from which to guide their lives. Regular face-to-face gatherings, not unlike friends gathering over coffee, book clubs, lunch bunches, and study groups, are essential.

At your gatherings, read aloud from "Becoming: Right for the Heart, Good for the Whole." Reflect on the reading, and share your reflections – your positive images of what could be... always remembering that since this is the work of the heart, there are no experts ...only wisdom to be shared.

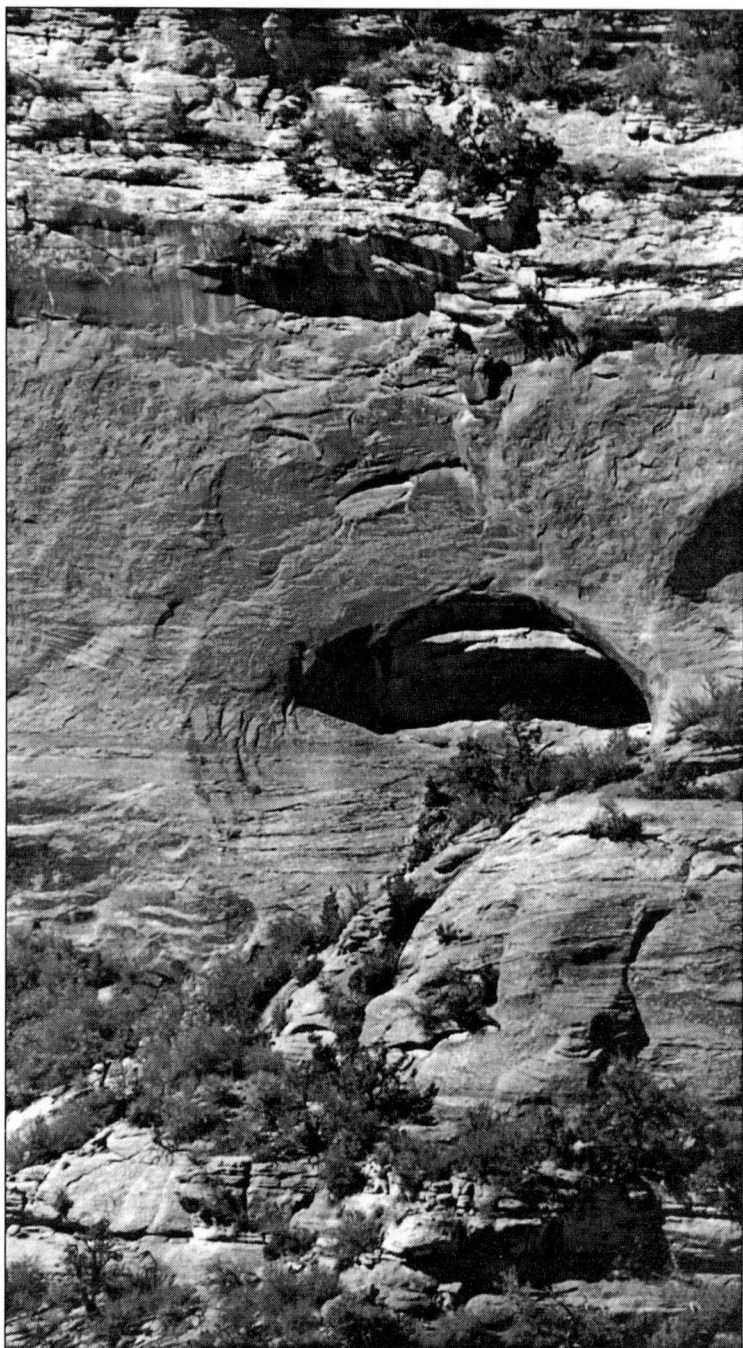

Path of Potential • P.O. Box 4058, Grand Junction, CO 81502 USA

Embracing the Truth of Our Oneness

- Contemplations -

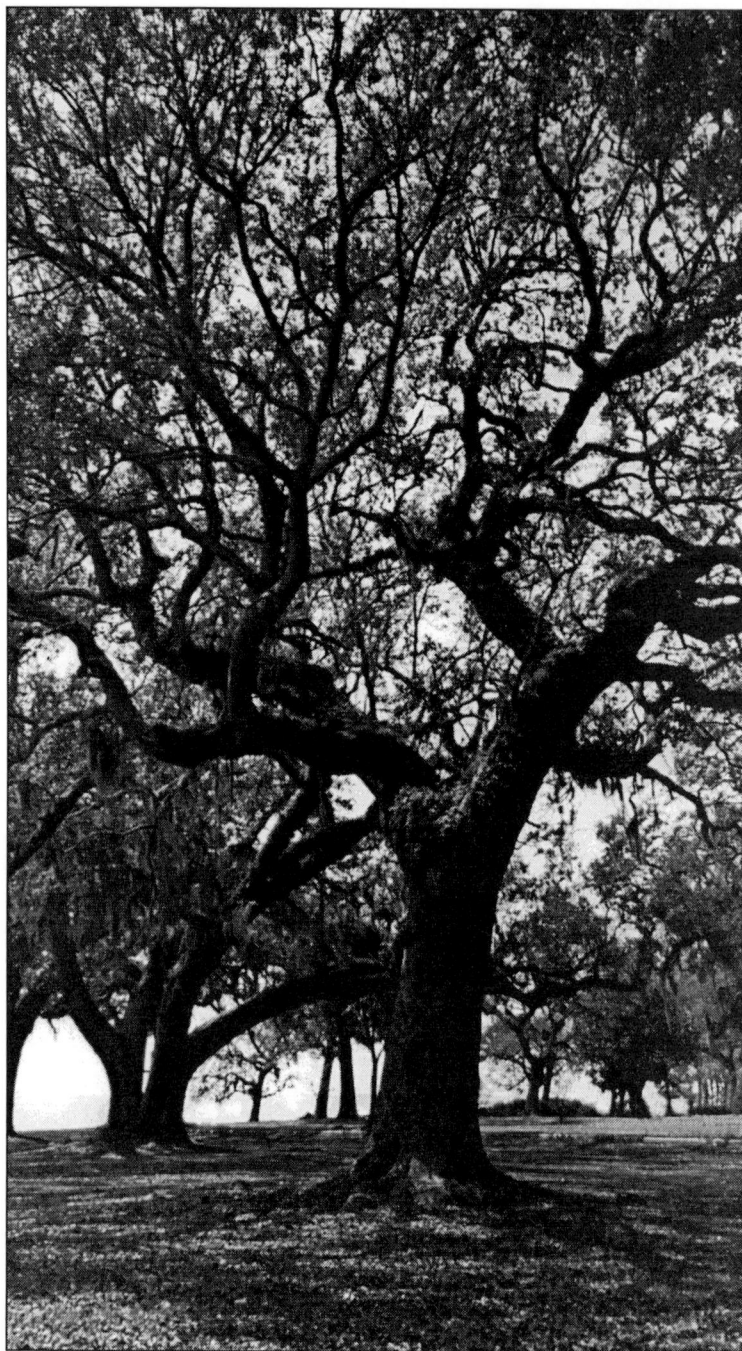

Path of Potential • P.O. Box 4058, Grand Junction, CO 81502 USA

Love must be in our processes.

Without love entering our hearts, there is...
*   no advancement toward humanness.*
*   no progress toward unity.*
*   no movement toward realizing our potential*
*   for becoming fully and truly human.*

Without love in our processes, there will be no love
in the outcomes.

Path of Potential • P.O. Box 4058, Grand Junction, CO 81502 USA

Love in the Process

If love is not present in the process, it will not be present in the outcomes.

We can remember the voices of our mothers and grandmothers, "Remember to salt the stew; if you forget the salt, no matter how much you sprinkle on at the end, it just never tastes the same." Like the essentiality of salt in the stew, love must be present in any process that has the aim of advancing us, lifting us up, moving us toward becoming more fully and truly human. As human beings, we have the potential to manifest our essence and uniqueness in ways that embrace, acknowledge and advance our oneness. Essence and uniqueness are called forth as we walk along the way toward realization - toward realizing our potential and becoming fully and truly human.

We see the necessity for love to be present in our processes as we reflect on one of the deepest of human hungers: the wish and the hope for a true and genuine peace... a peace not so much defined or bounded by an absence of violence (as great and wonderful as that would be), but rather a much richer, more spirited, more whole experience of being human:

- the experience of an inner sense of rightness and goodness.
- the experience of living and working in more dignified and inclusive ways.
- the experience of a more real - a more just - way for all.

Yes, peace on the way toward realization is experienced as a genuine advancement in our becoming more fully and truly human.

As we reflect and contemplate on peace, our thoughts naturally turn toward those who embraced this virtue and the nature of peace we long for. Of all the people who have walked this earth, the most notable, the ultimate exemplar is Christ. Christ is recognized well beyond those who call themselves Christian as the real and true exemplar of peace and, perhaps not surprisingly, love. There are others who sufficiently manifested the character and quality worthy of being called exemplars – inspiring sources for those who seek to pursue peace along the way toward realization. In recent times, four such exemplars are Mahatma Gandhi, Dr. Martin Luther King, Mother Teresa, and Pope John Paul II.

As we reflect on these exemplars, we notice there are some essential processes that are brought together in a systemic and dynamic way to produce, not only a base for, but a thrust and upward movement toward peace. We begin to see three processes inseparably integrated that work together in such a way that an uplifting, upward directed, peace emerges. These essential processes are...

- Walking in the spirit made manifest and exemplified by Christ... such a spirit manifested is available to all, forever.
- Holding within the heart the aim of accessing and acting from love – the love that emanates from the very essence of the Creator.
- Intentionally seeking to see and honor dignity – the dignity inherent in each and all.

One other thing shared by these exemplars is the deliberate, thoughtful, prayerful, contemplative process they engaged in before they acted. They seemed to grasp the necessity for seeing and understanding an essential truth - or truths - that would

Path of Potential • P.O. Box 4058, Grand Junction, CO 81502 USA

become the central focus, the very embodiment of themselves and their ways. They truly sought to become the change they were trying to bring about. And too, they seemingly understood that hazard accompanied even the highest of ways... hazard beyond the risk of one's life. The hazard for this nature of way is that those who would embrace it, and walk ever so diligently upon it, would begin to think of themselves as being the source rather than as intentional instruments, true participants, and co-creators.

Now, perhaps in the same vein as "Don't forget to salt the stew," we need to remind ourselves of another commonly experienced occurrence along the path. This occurrence seems to have the purpose of making us aware, or perhaps more accurately, of awakening us to situations that evoke within a real sense of wrongfulness - a strong enough sense that we experience ourselves becoming energized and drawn toward action. Through efforts by ourselves and others, motives – reasons and goals - begin to be generated. Energization and motivation are commonly joined by seeing the need for right-oriented control that shifts the wrongfulness toward right action and the right to act. When energization, motivation, and control rightfully work together, we often have a basis for and a direction toward the virtue of sharing power – more inclusivity.

Whereas engaging these situations may be less demanding than pursuing realization, they are in many ways much trickier to manage. This is especially true when we are "called to action" without the benefit of the deliberate, thoughtful, contemplative, prayerful process exhibited by our exemplars. If we cannot find a way to have love present in the process, we know that regardless of the apparent necessity or supposed merit, the "corrective action" will not advance us in our humanness.

Even with all of that, the hazard that seems to be the most detrimental to us as a people, and the larger impediment to our progress to becoming more fully and truly human, is the hazard of recycle... the pattern (which all too easily becomes habitual) of recycling the same situation – the pattern of our inability to move onward and upward. Through reflecting on our own experience (not very difficult, since virtually all of us are experienced swimmers in the waters of recycle), we do see some clues or indicators of recycling occurring. We notice that more and more, our energization takes on a deepening character of anger... anger that leads to disdain, and slides towards hatred. Motives and motivation begin to give way to demonization of others and desire for control – particularly legal control that works to impose rather than empower... and power rather than being shared and a source of greater access and inclusivity, turns toward hierarchical, positional, authoritative power over others. Ultimately power begins to corrupt.

Reflecting on what has been written here can produce within an overwhelming sense that can easily be accompanied by an inner tension... a tension which produces words like, "Oh yes ... but no." Yet in the face of the realness of what we can see, understand and experience lies much hope. We, each and all, have within dignity. Dignity is intentionally, inherently within our design as human beings. As such, it is accessible, knowable and manifestable. Dignity opens up for us the accessing of spirit and love. It both provides a way for us to break the cycle of recycle, and to take on a real role on the way toward our becoming fully and truly human. Such a role requires (not power, but rather) an open heart... a heart open and welcoming to spirit and love; one imbued with

Path of Potential • P.O. Box 4058, Grand Junction, CO 81502 USA

seeing and honoring dignity... a heart willing to take on a role working in ways that honor and celebrate our essence and uniqueness while faithfully and deliberately striving to stay on the way.

Work is the means by which
we fulfill our purpose,
realize our potential,
and manifest the dignity that lies within.

Path of Potential • P.O. Box 4058, Grand Junction, CO 81502 USA

Our Choice

If we choose love as our Source...

> We walk, regardless of the size of our steps, along the path of our Creator.

> Wisdom and understanding lie along our path.

> Understanding reveals to us the truth of our design.

> We see that each of us, all people, share a common Father.

> Each and all are intended to be manifestations of essence gifts and truth.

> We discover the truth of our oneness as a human family... and the truth of our membership in the community of life - life that springs from and is continuously nourished by mother earth.

> Through understanding, compassion becomes possible... a compassion that grows through the revelation of the commonness of our struggle.

> Compassion through understanding is the ongoing source of hope.

Like all of life's members,
we too have a role
in the working of the whole
of which we are a part.

Path of Potential • P.O. Box 4058, Grand Junction, CO 81502 USA

The Story of
Our Experience and Heritage

In the beginning,
our very first act of disobedience
was to interfere with the intended
working of the world...

In the beginning, at the earliest of human times... through the intentional act of the Creator... there emerged from the earth, a people – a living people of earth. The people enjoyed an unending abundance, constant happiness, and real peace. A harmony existed among all the creatures of earth.

At the start of the beginning, the intention of the Creator was made known. The Creator put forth instructions or laws by which the people were to live in community. Now the people, being unique among life's creatures, could choose to obey or not to obey the Creator's laws. The people, by design, were endowed with free will – and as such were not subject to the automatic behavior and obedience practiced by the other creatures of earth. Somewhere along the way, temptation became ever more present. Succumbing to this temptation, the people chose to act from themselves, rather than live in accord with the Creator's instructions.

The people became increasingly knowledgeable, but decreasingly wise. More and more they used their knowledge to serve themselves; less and less regard did they have for the Creator's intention. As time passed - as they progressed along their chosen path – the people began to experience illness, sorrow, war, strife, woe and emptiness... the opposite of the beginning. Earth, the very home of life itself, became threatened.

That was then...

Now is now.

The past is past... the future is yet to unfold. Now is the time to uncover a new path – a new way of being.

> The people are beginning to awaken.
> Conscience is being stirred to life.
> Love is seeking to enter.
> Hearts are opening themselves to wisdom.
> Intuition is coming into play.

> There is a growing sense of a calling...
>> A call to reclaim our heritage...
>>> our heritage of peace and
>>> wholeness...
>> A call to fulfill our role.

> An ethic is striving to emerge...
> An ethic for living wisely on this earth...
> An ethic born from essential truths...
>> ... the truth of our being a people of
>> earth.
>> ... the truth of our shared humanness.
>> ... the truth of our being members of the
>> community of life.
>> ... the truth of our common Source.
>> ... the truth of our calling to become
>> fully and truly human.
>> ... the truth that all are called, and each
>> may choose.

Humankind
has a role
in the work
and working
of the life processes
of earth.

*No one person
is above another -
we are in truth,
in spirit,
in essence,
and in dignity,
equal.*

Path of Potential • P.O. Box 4058, Grand Junction, CO 81502 USA

Fully and Truly Human

We are becoming FULLY human when we are...
- Seeing and living from essence and the truth of our oneness – oneness with humanity, oneness with life, oneness with earth, and oneness with the Source of creation.
- Seeking and honoring the dignity in each and all.
- Living from and manifesting spirit.

We are becoming TRULY human when we realize...
- We are not the source, but rather the instruments.
- We are members of life – and as members, we must embrace the stages and phases of life (our lives) and the realness of death.
- We have roles to play, work to do – thus purpose and meaning.
- We each are unique - having potential to be realized.
- We have within the capacity to access and manifest spirit.
- We are capable of understanding the intent and design.
- Inner and outer peace are both realizable and intended.
- We, humankind, are not the center of all, but an essential part of life-of-the-whole.

Through reflection
we are given
the gift of "seeing"
what could be for each and for all.

Path of Potential • P.O. Box 4058, Grand Junction, CO 81502 USA

Entering the Sphere of Dignity

There is an Australian Aboriginal principle of not camping near a waterhole. The Aboriginal people see themselves as members of a community of life. As such, they honor and understand the need for all members to have free access to the waterhole. They understand access as being critical not only to individual survival, but to the effective working of the processes of life itself.

We can see in the wisdom of this principle that we, all of humanity, have within us the character of being members of a living community; we are a systemic element in the whole of life. Like all of life's members, and in particular life's systems, we too have a role in the working of the whole of which we are a part: a role that has as a central element the accountability and responsibility for sustaining life, life processes, and the regenerative capacity of the living systems and planetary energy fields of earth... a role that requires us to live in concert with the principle of the waterhole.

We see also in this principle the inherent truth of our dignity. We have each been designed with dignity and possess within us the capacity to dignify; we all share a common thirst to realize this dignity. As is true for the waterhole, we cannot pursue satiating our thirst for dignity at the expense of our fellow humans... or fellow members of life. At the same time, we can see within dignity, the possibility for a space into which all of humanity, all of life can enter. In the same manner in which all of life nourishes itself at the waterhole, we, the people, regardless of race, creed, place of origin, etc., can enter this place – this sphere of dignity – that has as its aim honoring the essence and uniqueness of each and all, and a common purpose of realizing the open-ended potential that lies within. In so doing, we can continue along the path of becoming fully and truly human.

Like all being and becoming decisions, this decision to honor the all-inclusive space of dignity requires free and conscious choice. Such a choice would be an act of faith and an act of hope: faith in the intentional design of our humanness, and hope because this sphere of dignity, not unlike the waterhole, is a place where ALL of humanity and ALL of life can enter.

We, each and all, have within dignity.

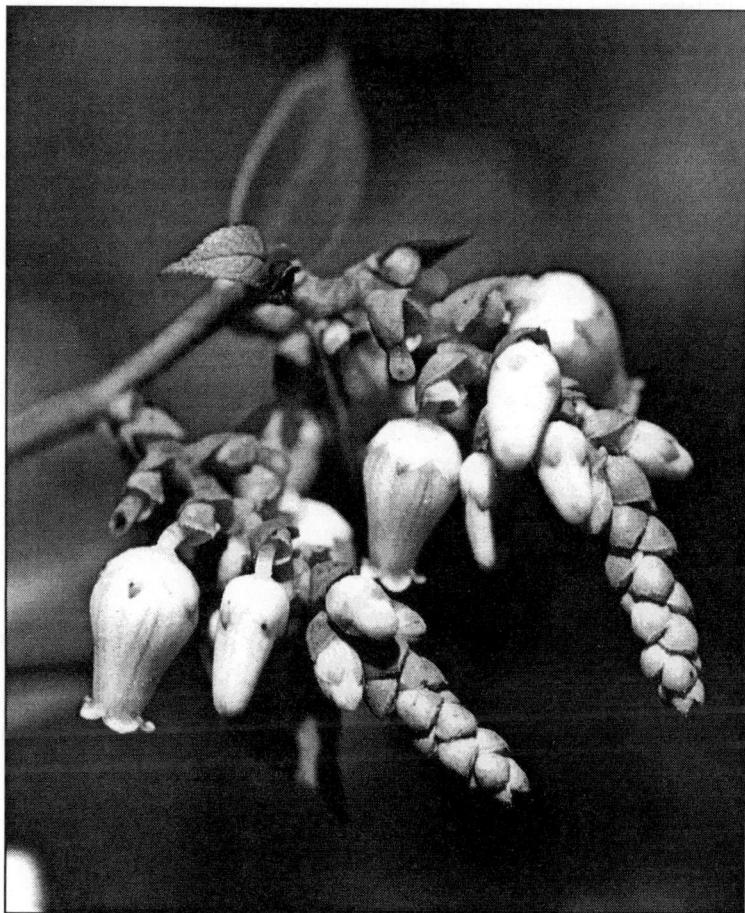

Elevating Dignity through Work

As with earth and its life processes, it is also readily apparent that work is an essential life process, inherent in the design and intent of the thread of life we call humankind. We can see it at play in the duality of our existence and essence. Work is the means by which we advance the value of things - the means by which we generate economics... hopefully favorable economics. From the essence aspect of our life, work is the process by which we manifest our uniqueness and essence. Work is the means for bringing forth and realizing open-ended potential. Work provides the opportunity to manage the realities of our existence and the possibility of living out the destiny that lies within essence and potential. At its core, work is an integrating process – it calls upon our will while integrating our being into our doing; likewise it integrates essence into our existence. It is the means by which we embed character and qualities into that which we produce. It is through work, and its associated roles, that we gain a sense of purpose to our lives – a true sense that we can make a difference. Likewise, work is the means by which humankind can fulfill its purpose, realize its potential, and manifest the dignity that lies within.

We know we are on course if dignity is being elevated in and through our work. For it is through dignifying that we become fully and truly human; if dignity declines, our very humanness declines... and humanity disappears.

Dignity opens up for us
the accessing of
spirit and love.

We have each been designed
with dignity... and possess
within us the capacity
to dignify.

Path of Potential • P.O. Box 4058, Grand Junction, CO 81502 USA

Be Gentle, People of Earth

What does it mean to be gentle? To be gentle is to interact in a way that the other is able to be what it is struggling to be, and become what is in its most inner – its most essential – nature to become. To be gentle is to allow and enable all of this while interacting with anything that has life in it. Be gentle with precious life.

Be gentle when pruning a tree; be gentle when feeding a baby; be gentle when disciplining a pet; be gentle when walking in the desert; be gentle when caring for the dying; be gentle when assisting a birthing; be gentle when picking a flower; be gentle when teaching a child; be gentle when loving your spouse; be gentle when gathering fruit and grain; be gentle when exploring the earth; be gentle when building a home.

Be gentle... for when we are gentle with life, life's processes, life's systems, and life's resources, then we will belong to earth and earth will belong to us. We become one; we become whole... we become one whole. We will possess earth as a parent "possesses" a child: we will have access to the joy it has to offer, while we have responsibility to bring to it our love and full force of caring.

Gentleness is the instrument through which the Creator's love can flow to the work of perfection and completeness of life. Gentleness is the means by which we become real and true members of earth... of life of the whole.

Reflections on the Worlds of Humankind

Humankind has three worlds from which to draw and into which we may enter and operate. Each of these worlds has within it a fundamental truth from which all other truths emanate. The first of these is the World of Will. The fundamental truth of this world is that there is a Source: A Creative Force, an Ultimate Will that is the Source of all creation. The second of these is the World of Essence, essence being the pattern of potentialities for each and all - for all and everything that has been created. The truth of the World of Essence is the unboundedness of open-ended potential. In this world humankind can experience freedom from limitations of time and material. In the World of Will, humankind can experience a truth expressed generations ago by Christ: "With God all things are possible." In the World of Essence, humankind can experience and embrace the limitlessness of open-ended potential.

The third world is the World of Existence. The World of Existence holds within it that which has been manifested and is detectable through the senses. This includes the seemingly invisible energies of formation and energies of interaction. The fundamental truth of existence is life. The World of Existence has as its core, as its central focus, life and life generating processes. Humankind, although it may truly represent life's most developed form – even to the extent of being developed in the image and likeness of the Creator – is without a doubt a participant in the whole of a process greater than humankind... that of life. As is true of all other participants, and therefore it would be expected to be true for humankind, humankind has a

Path of Potential • P.O. Box 4058, Grand Junction, CO 81502 USA

role in the work and working of the life processes of earth - a role that fulfills the intent and design of the Creator. The Creator's intent has been expressed as one of humankind having dominion over earth and being a co-creator. Reflecting on our design and the unfolding developmental processes in which humankind is engaged, it is becoming increasingly apparent that humankind's role, our ultimate role, is to carry out the Will of the Creator in the World of Existence. Humankind's co-creative role is to enable the life-driven evolutionary processes of which man is a part; we are called to be the managing stewards of the whole of existence. Although we are not yet fully developed and capable of fulfilling this role, it is within our existing design, and therefore intended. The means for realizing our potential and fulfilling the intent and design of the Creator has been shown to us.

*We are intended and designed as instruments
with authentic and genuine roles in the unfolding,
and yet to be unfolded majesty
and mystery of creation.*

Path of Potential • P.O. Box 4058, Grand Junction, CO 81502 USA

The Dot and the Line

The dot and the line are an appropriate symbol for an essential truth critical to our time. The dot represents the Creator, and the line represents all else. The fundamental truth being that only the Creator is above – the dot is the sole domain of the Creator. All else – particularly, each and every one of us – dwell on the same line, the same plane. No one person is above another person – we are in truth, in spirit, in essence, and in dignity, equal. Each and all belong to the human family, and by intentional design, also belong to the greater community of life.

We, humankind, have a long history of effort and energy expended to create positional differentiations within the line. It is common for people to strive to gain "higher position," and seek and enjoy the status that accompanies that position. In truth and in essence, there are differentiations within the context of the dot and the line that are both real and necessary. These differentiations reflect the truth of our equality and are manifested, not in position, but rather through roles that are required to carry out our work of sustaining and advancing the processes essential to our becoming fully and truly human... roles that not only reflect our instrumentality, but also ones that acknowledge the realness of the work to be done and the significance of our part.

Within the shifting of our effort and attention away from hierarchical position and personal advantage towards work sourced in and aimed at the sustaining, development, and evolution of these essential processes, life for us becomes very real. We shift from positions of importance to roles of significance... roles that require the discovery and manifestation of essence and uniqueness. Work becomes a source of meaning and dignity in our lives. We find we are not so much desiring dignity and rights, but rather experiencing the dignity and nobility inherent within our design as we seek and pursue the right and good. Structures, structuring and organizing emerge that serve the right and good working of essential processes. Wisdom and reason, imbued with faith and powered by love, are aligned and conscientiously, consciously, and harmoniously working with the intentional design and unfolding plan of creation. Truthful, spirit-lifting answers become possible to the innermost questions of humankind: Am I living a life I believe in? What is the purpose for which I was created and to which I am called? What is my role in the work and working of the community of humanity? What is my role in the work and working of the community of life?

Path of Potential • P.O. Box 4058, Grand Junction, CO 81502 USA

The Gift of Imaging

From the Creator flows love.

When we open our hearts to the flow of the Creator's love, that love enters us and reflects back to us images of "what could be" - what is intended to be... what we ourselves could become, and the becoming of life itself - a becoming of life of the whole in which we are called to play our role. Through reflection - through opening our hearts to the everlasting flow of love of the Creator - we are given the gift of "seeing" - seeing "what could be" for each and for all. We know that "seeing" is a gift of the Creator when the image of "what could be" is neither self-centered nor human-centered, but life-of-the-whole-centered - where each member of life and all members of life are elevated - inspirited - within the image... and we - each and all - have a role we can play that participates in bringing that image into being. In this way, we become participating players in the ongoing creation... and by so doing, fulfill the longing to become with which we were designed.

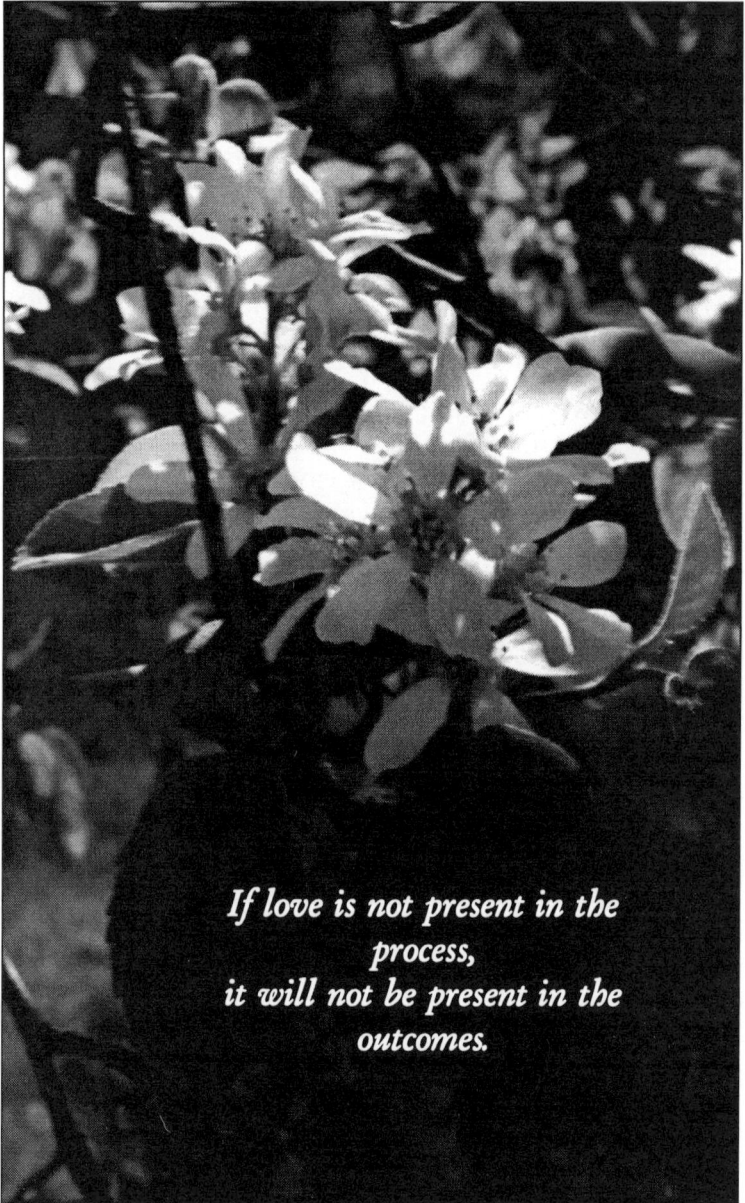

If love is not present in the process,
it will not be present in the outcomes.

Path of Potential • P.O. Box 4058, Grand Junction, CO 81502 USA

Life-Giving Joy of Spirit

Spirit allows us to move beyond the world of material – beyond existence – to the world of essence...

Spirit awakens in us a search for deeper meaning – beyond the desire for answers, corrective action, or retribution...

Spirit entering into a receptive heart makes possible the seeing of essential purpose, our calling, and our reason for being...

It is Spirit that brings joy to life by lighting the path of each, all and everything.

Spirit brings life to our life, for spirit is the life force - the Source of all life...

Spirit is the way to see the truth of our existence; it is the source of meaning and purpose for our lives and for the whole of life...

Spirit is wisdom in action - the means for fulfilling the will of our Creator...

Spirit brings questioning that builds hope and dissipates despair.

Wherever spirit is manifested, so too life is present.

When spirit leaves, life is gone... yet spirit returns when it finds a receptive heart through which to enter.

A receptive heart through which spirit flows into the world and into life is available forever to all as an eternal instrument.

Building the Soul of Humanity

The manifested will of the Creator is actively and busily at work... tirelessly and unceasingly working to advance the work of the Creator. This work is work we cannot do, but work that cannot be done unless we are... are what we need to be such that spirit, and therefore love, can enter into and flow through the life processes of earth.

We are being called not to be in control of nor to have control over, but rather to cooperate with; not so much to lead, but rather to be led - led by the images that enter the heart receptive to wisdom and guided by the light of our conscience. This work demands unbending resolve and ever deepening patience on our part, for this work holds as its aim an unfolding - an unfolding with which we are fully able to cooperate. But also this work is one which we - as of yet - lack the capacity to fully envision, to see the whole, and the processes therein.

This is work not of the one, but of the many. Hope is active and entering all those with receptive hearts - hearts that long to become instruments, hearts that are striving to be free of the illusion of being a or the source. As hope enters and establishes its presence by flowing through, images and envisionments born of love become visible and accessible - images that make possible the seeing of our role - our path - and the clarifying of our work - work that is both a manifestation of essence, and the hopeful intent of our Creator.

While the whole of that which is to be brought about is not yet visible to us, what is being illuminated is the process of building the soul of humanity. This is the

Path of Potential • P.O. Box 4058, Grand Junction, CO 81502 USA

work that is required for humankind – the human race – to become fully and truly human, and thereby capable of fulfilling its intended role in the working of the world. This soul building work - this effort to prepare us for our intended role – calls upon the uniqueness of each and all, and requires the working and manifesting of spirit through our essence. This is the means; this is the process; this is the work before us.

Let us pray that we will not be tempted by illusions of "being the source," of being "in charge of," nor by the pursuit of "control over." May our faith in the intent and design of the Creator ever strengthen and grow imperturbably within us. May we have the strength of resolve that becomes possible only through the desire to carry out "Thy Will." May the spirit and love of the Creator find ever increasing numbers of receptive hearts to enter and to flow through... such that the love required for manifesting the intentional unfolding is truly present.

*Love must be present
in any process that
has the aim of
moving us toward
becoming more
fully and truly
human.*

Path of Potential • P.O. Box 4058, Grand Junction, CO 81502 USA

Reflections on Wholeness

Wholeness is a manifestation of the working of truths. It is the experience of our inner being when we are open to truths - with the ultimate truth and the Source of all truths being love. Wholeness is both a deep sense of connectedness to the Source, and an experiential understanding of the truth of our intended participation in the process of creation.

Wholeness is both a process and a manifestation of a process. It is a state of being that, while unlimited in scope and depth, deepens in meaning as our living and working become increasingly harmonious with our purpose and the core processes of our socio-eco community. It is not capture-able in the sense that we can possess it; in many ways, it is similar to the ebb and flow of the tides.

We notice wholeness diminishes - it flows away from us - as we lose sight of the right and good working of the larger wholes of which we are a part: the human family, the whole of life. It retreats when we retreat into ourselves - particularly into the serving of ourselves. It flows into and through us as we remember and act from our instrumentality. It flows into and through us when we source our thoughts (and therefore the path we take) in our essential roles and purposes, and in the potential they offer to our becoming fully and truly human.

Wholeness is the work of the heart as it embraces both our oneness and our individuality; it reconciles and elevates both. It is what draws us toward and reveals more clearly the truth of our oneness and the reality of our uniqueness. Wholeness is the means by which we progress - as individuals, as communities, as the human family. It is a requirement for the taking on and fulfilling of our essential roles - roles within the human family, and roles within the whole of life.

Wholeness is achievable not through the resolution of differences, but rather in the pursuit of higher purposes, the celebration of uniqueness, and the manifestation of essences. If we (individually or communally) lose sight of higher purpose and pursue other than essential purposes, wholeness dissipates. Wholeness is not about the imposition of one's will or perceived rights; it is about the surrendering to one's instrumentality... the instrumentality that lies within and emanates from the intent and design of the Creator.

Path of Potential • P.O. Box 4058, Grand Junction, CO 81502 USA

*Love's working
calls upon
and requires
open receptive hearts
and willful instruments.*

Truly Living Our Lives

Reflecting on the interesting and ancient phrase, "to spare our life," we see there are many ways we try to spare our lives. One is to avoid experiencing life. We avoid experiencing life by accommodating our irrational fears, by refusing to learn or try something new in fear of failure or embarrassment, by reconciling to old and established patterns of doing and being (justifying ourselves with "that is the way I am") by ignoring the glimpses of wisdom given to us in quiet reflective moments; instead we operate to cultural norms and values not in tune with our true self. Yes, there are endless ways in which we seem to keep ourselves from experiencing life.

We also spare our lives by ignoring our heart... sparing ourselves the anxiety and inner turmoil that come when we stand for and live from what our heart tells us is good... that is, the common good, not merely the convenient better. To come from the heart, we reflect on our inner core... we make a reflective effort to see the essence of our design, then work to manifest that essential self in all that we are and in all that we do.

We spare our lives by ignoring rather than pursuing the intent for which we were created - our purpose within the whole of creation. Accepting and embracing our essential purpose, we cannot spare our life. Each of us has our own unique calling: the particular purpose we were designed and intended to pursue during our life... and that purpose is beyond our life, beyond self, beyond humanity. That purpose calls upon us to play a role that serves a larger whole... which serves an aspect of the creation process itself.

There is a pattern to all callings: *To live out and harmonize with a particular virtue (make it manifest in the*

Path of Potential • P.O. Box 4058, Grand Junction, CO 81502 USA

world)... in a way that elevates the common good... so that a particular aspect of the Creator's plan continues in its unfolding. Our calling requires we forfeit the life we had for a new life – a life in which we - in heart, body and mind – seek to become a truly working and wholly present element in a larger system... a system that is working to keep alive the ongoing manifestation of a virtue pouring into this earth from the Creator.

Yes, it does seem that if we choose to spare our life, we will lose it... yet if we give it up to our calling, we will truly experience what it means to be alive.

Wholeness is the work of the heart
as it embraces both our oneness
and our individuality.

Path of Potential • P.O. Box 4058, Grand Junction, CO 81502 USA

Reflecting on the Working of Love

Love… continuously emanates from the Essence of creation, its true and only Source. With unfailing alertness and infinite patience, love seeks an opening through which it can flow… the means by which it can enter into the working of the world. In the absence of an open vessel, a receptive heart, love cannot enter the world… and a loveless world ceases to work, ceases to be, and brings unimaginable suffering to its Creator.

Upon entry, love works not to gain power… nor does it pursue power and authority over others; it seeks not to dominate, nor to be understood. Love seeks to illuminate and gain understanding of.

Love casts not shadows… it is pure light… a light that freely enters a receptive heart - a beckoning instrument. Love, once welcomed, goes about its work of reflecting from and among one another… a reflecting that awakens faith, breathes life into hope, and strengthens spirit. Love illuminates ultimate truths… the truth of our instrumentality… the illusion of our being a source… the truth of our oneness and equality… the reality that but for our Creator, no one is superior. Love celebrates our uniqueness as it works to unfold and manifest our essence.

While love holds salvation as its purpose… love has as its ultimate aim lighting the path of evolution of our being… the path by which we ultimately become that which was and is intended: a perfect reflection of the image from and through which we were created. Love enters and lights our path in ways that sustain our longing to return and our ever-strengthening yearning to become. Always beckoning and occasionally admonishing us along our intended path of progression, love lightens the burden of our soul... yet calls attention to and provides focus to the work before us.

Love lights the way... and leads us to advance our humanness beyond love based on or restricted to common or shared blood... to embrace one another, each and all members of the human family, as brothers and sisters – neighbors, one and all.

As we, humankind, progress along our path, and our capacity for embracing the working of love deepens, our work becomes increasingly intrinsic... requiring more inner acceptance and a freer and more conscious choice not realizable through external forces (i.e., authority or persuasion, reason and logical argument, commands, threats, fear or guilt), but more and more through the work of our heart and the working of our conscience. Each new progression does not diminish the significance of the previous, nor lessen it being required... rather, that which comes before becomes enfolded into the new... with deeper and truer meaning, and a greater possibility of being truly lived out. Thus the new progression - to embrace the whole of life, to understand and honor its working, and to nourish and bring forth life's potential and its processes - does not diminish the love required and intended between and among our brothers and sisters... nor does it lessen, but rather makes more real, the truth of our dignity and equality. And, as we continue our progression along our path, love's working calls upon and requires many more, not fewer, receptive hearts and willful instruments... especially now, with oneness and wholeness being brought to the fore. These receptive hearts become the focal points of the light, of that which is to be understood and served... the aim of our work.

     Path of Potential • P.O. Box 4058, Grand Junction, CO 81502 USA

By tuning into the virtue of the land, we are able to transcend divisiveness, celebrate uniquenesses, and through community, experience and generate wholeness - the aim and expression of the truth of our oneness.

Path of Potential • P.O. Box 4058, Grand Junction, CO 81502 USA

That which love illuminates and wisdom
enables us to see, brings to faith
a new dimension and added perspective.
Faith which has worked to
sustain the path of our return and salvation
now adds the dimension of our instrumentality
and role in the ongoing creation...
for humankind was not intended nor designed
as the end point of creation,
but rather as an instrument with an authentic and
genuine co-creator role...
a role in the unfolding, and yet to be unfolded
majesty and mystery of creation...
a role that requires we become
fully and truly human...
thus fulfilling and perfecting the intent
and design of the Creator...
and therein lies the hope.

Titles by Path of Potential

- Becoming - *Right for the Heart... Good for the Whole*
- Building Your Life Philosophy - *Food for Thought*
- Dignity through Essence
- Earth Speaking
- Gifts of the Spirit - *Experiencing Death and Loss from the Perspective of Potential.*
- Love at Work
- Our Choice
- Shedding Burdens
- Taking Youth Work to Heart
- The Practice of Potential - *Working from Images*
- Wholeness - *Working Aim of Life*
- Work for all Children - *Parenting Reflections from the Perspective of Potential*
- Work of the Heart
- Working with Meaning

Path of Potential

Path of Potential is a 501(c)(3) Nonprofit Corporation dedicated to making visible the perspective of potential through publishing books and readers, maintaining a free website, and leading reflective dialogues for creating practical living philosophies and purposes.

The work of Path of Potential is supported by contributions and supplemented by proceeds from book and reader sales and subscriptions.

For additional information about the work of **Path of Potential** or it's publications, visit our website at www.pathofpotential.org , write to **Path of Potential**, P.O. Box 4058, Grand Junction, CO 81502 USA, or email: editor@pathofpotential.org.